Managing
and
Leading
Well

**It Ain't Rocket Science,
But It's Still Hard Work!**

Managing
and
Leading
Well

It Ain't Rocket Science, But It's Still Hard Work!

B. Dan Berger
and
Anthony W. Demangone

NAFCU | National Association of Federal Credit Unions

Managing and Leading Well:
It Ain't Rocket Science, But It's Still Hard Work!
By B. Dan Berger and Anthony W. Demangone

Copyright © 2014, NAFCU

Published by National Association of Federal Credit Unions
3138 10th Street North, Arlington, Virginia 22201
800-336-4644 • www.nafcu.org

Edited by Jay Morris Communications LLC
Alexandria, Virginia

Designed by Spectrum Creative LLC
Fairfax, Virginia

ISBN: 978-0-9903037-0-1

Printed and manufactured in the United States of America

First Printing, June 2014

Contents

Contents

Foreword

When Dan Berger and Anthony Demangone told me they were writing a book about management and leadership, I got very excited.

You see, I have a passion for teaching leadership essentials. I've written books, given talks and conducted management-training workshops at organizations across the globe.

No matter where I go or whom I talk to, I find that people want to be better leaders and managers. They're hungry for basic knowledge and skills. There's a real need for books and seminars that teach leadership in a straightforward, practical way and cut through the clutter to focus on the fundamentals.

That's what I like about Dan and Anthony's book. They make leadership accessible, understandable and achievable.

I easily read over 100 business books a year, and I have to say that Dan and Anthony are spot on with their book.

Reading through their chapters, I was delighted to discover everything I've studied and lectured about over the years. Change. Vision. Communication. Attitude. Collaboration. Learning. Trust. Accountability. Execution. It's all there. And they did it in one, very readable book!

Make no mistake, there is a real need for leadership development in today's business environment. Harvard Business Publishing recently surveyed over 800 executives and talent development professionals and found that only 32 percent believe that their organization has the right leadership skills to achieve its strategic goals.

Eighty percent of the respondents said that their middle managers need to develop change management capabilities.

In my own research, I've identified four key leadership challenges. These are the top issues that I hear about over and over when I meet with clients. They are what hold organizations back and keep CEOs up at night.

1. Lack of a vivid and extremely well-communicated vision.
2. Lack of open, honest and courageous communication.
3. Lack of accountability.
4. Lack of disciplined execution.

Here's my promise: If you take the time to read this book, you'll be armed with the tools to meet these challenges head on.

As Dan and Anthony would say, "It ain't rocket science, but it's still hard work!"

So go ahead and start reading!

John Spence

John Spence is the author of Awesomely Simple *and* Excellence by Design: Leadership. *He is an internationally recognized lecturer, trainer and consultant on leadership, management and motivation. For the past two decades, he has traveled worldwide to assist more than 300 client companies such as Microsoft, IBM, Apple, GE, Qualcomm and numerous other Fortune 500 firms.*

Acknowledgments

We gratefully thank the NAFCU Board of Directors for providing us with the strategic direction and support to be successful in what we do. We thank our NAFCU credit union members for inspiring us each and every day, reminding us of how great an industry it is we serve. We thank the incredible NAFCU staff, who provide "Extreme Member Service" day in and day out, and help our members thrive in an increasingly competitive marketplace. We give a big shout-out to Jay Morris, one of the best editors and scribes to walk this planet. Finally, we both would be in the doghouse if we didn't thank our families for their continued love and support, especially for the long hours and days we've spent away from home.

Dan & Anthony

Introduction

Go ahead, thumb through the pages of our book. Inspect its table of contents. It's okay, we know the drill.

You want to know why you should read this book, right? We don't blame you.

After all, why should you invest time with us when there are so many other things you could be doing?

Well, here's one good reason right off the bat: This book was written for you. It has your name all over it. And while you may not know it just yet, you *need* this book. In fact, you'll thank us when you're done reading it. That's our little guarantee.

First, a little bit about us. We're two guys who care a great deal about credit unions. We're absolutely passionate about providing extreme service to NAFCU members and creating a culture that can deliver on that promise. We also know a lot about the issues that affect your operation, issues that we diligently champion on your behalf before Congress, the NCUA and other regulatory agencies.

There's no doubt that compliance occupies your time—more time than it should, in our judgment. You spend days and nights worrying about the latest NCUA regulations and what the Fed, Treasury or CFPB will do next. We understand, and we feel your pain.

Needed: More People Skills

But did you know that there is another threat to our industry equally as serious as the compliance burden you wrestle with daily? It might be even more insidious because it's often overlooked.

What could it be, you ask?

Quite simply, people.

People?

That's right, people. More specifically, **managing and leading people** so that your credit union can survive and thrive in this hypercompetitive and highly regulated marketplace.

Let's face it, running a credit union isn't easy, and lately it seems like it's getting even harder.

Day after day, you're giving it your all. You're working hard to serve your members, comply with burdensome regulations and compete head-to-head with the largest of financial institutions.

You're looking for that edge that will help you better lead your people and build winning teams. In short, you need to be at the top of your management game.

If you're a credit union CEO, think about how you came up in the ranks. Do you have a degree in accounting or finance? Were you a vice president of lending? A CFO?

Did you receive any formal management or leadership training?

Most of us have had a lot of specialized training, whether it's in finance, accounting or operations, but few of us have been taught *how to lead*.

Critics sometimes point to a "leadership deficit" in our industry. Think about your own credit union. Are you developing your people?

We know it's not easy. We struggle with the same things.

And we're not alone. The first chapter in our book deals with change management. Change is hard work, and management experts say that one of the biggest reasons why change doesn't take hold in organizations is because CEOs universally fail to appreciate that change only occurs when people embrace it.

This basic failure to understand people and what motivates them occurs in *all* industries. That's because many CEOs, no matter the organization, are good at process, but not so good at leading people.

How High Is Your EQ?

It brings to mind Daniel Goleman's seminal book, *Emotional Intelligence*, which popularized the concept of EQ, or emotional intelligence, as a determining factor in management success.

We like Goleman's book and his 1998 *Harvard Business Review* article because his research makes clear that traditional qualities associated with leadership such as intelligence, technical skills and determination are not enough for success. Truly effective leaders are distinguished by a high degree of emotional intelligence, which includes self-awareness, self-regulation, motivation, empathy and social skill.

Goleman studied 200 large global companies and discovered that EQ was twice as important as IQ and technical skills for success at *all* job levels.

It sounds a bit like the old right-brain-versus-left-brain behavior model, doesn't it? Leadership requires balancing the tendency to think rationally and sequentially (left brain) with imagination, creativity, empathy and play (right brain).

In fact, those right-brain skills may be more important than we realized. Research by the Carnegie Institute of Technology shows that 85 percent of our financial success is due to personality and our ability to communicate, negotiate and lead. Only 15 percent is due to technical knowledge!

As Daniel Pink writes persuasively in *A Whole New Mind*, the world is changing, and right-brainers are on the ascendancy. We once needed an army of programmers, engineers and lawyers, but today we need more artists, inventors and designers. The Information Age is giving way to the Conceptual Age, and with that shift comes changes in the way we look at leadership.

The aptitudes that Pink identifies as being important in this new Conceptual Age are the very ones we're seeing in Gen X and Y workers and younger credit union members: an appreciation for design, storytelling, seeing the big picture, understanding and caring about others, having fun and creating joy, and finding meaning in work.

Wanted: More Right-Brain Knowledge

Astute credit union leaders know the times are changing; they know they need to acquire and teach these new "soft skills" in order to stay in the game. Everywhere we go, credit union people tell us they are thirsty for management and leadership advice.

NAFCU has always been a leader in the legislative, regulatory and compliance arena. Our members rely on us for left-brain intelligence. Now they are saying they need more right-brain knowledge to be competitive.

So this is the reason for our book: We want our members—the whole credit union industry really—to be prepared and equipped to lead. We want leaders with passion. Leaders who embrace change rather than avoid it. Leaders who are good with numbers but also have vision and creative solutions.

You may think that's a tall order, but we think it's doable. We also believe that the tools are already out there in abundance. They just need to be applied.

We both read a lot of business and leadership books. Most make very similar points about building winning teams and motivating people. And while they may not always be original, they do energize and renew us. They keep us on track and remind us of fundamentals that we may have forgotten. They're like a good coach, a caring parent or concerned mentor.

This book, then, is not about imparting never-before-revealed "secrets" of management. Think of it as a guide, a straightforward and honest companion as you strive to better lead the people in your credit union.

As we said in the beginning, you *need* this book. We all need this book because leadership and management skills take practice. Leadership is like a muscle that needs to be exercised. It requires effort and repetition. Even world-class athletes have to practice and hone their skills.

Managing and leading well—it ain't rocket science, but it's still hard work. So let's get started!

Dan & Anthony

CHAPTER ONE

Change

*"The only way to make sense out of change is to
plunge into it, move with it, and join the dance."*
– ALAN WATTS

Wouldn't it be nice if we knew when change
was about to happen? Like in a Western,
when the bad guys ride into town and there's plenty
of foreshadowing. If we knew there was a black swan
event coming, the kind that Nassim Nicholas Taleb
wrote about in his best-selling book, we could get
ready, right?

Some changes we do know about, and we can anticipate them. For example, both of us are fathers, and
though we might not be prepared for every aspect
of parenthood (like a surprise visit to the emergency

room), we know something about growing up. We know from our own experience, family members, friends and all kinds of cultural references what's in store—for the most part.

By the same token, credit union leaders know a lot about the kinds of changes that affect their institutions, and they can anticipate those, too. They have lots of information from NCUA and NAFCU's research department.

There is market research to find out more about members and their financial needs. There are annual strategic planning sessions. In short, there is plenty of information out there.

But having a lot of information at our fingertips doesn't always mean we're ready for change, especially transformational change. Nor does it mean that we're prepared for the black swan events that "come out of the blue" and that no one really could have anticipated—game-changing events that disrupt markets and turn our lives upside down.

Moore's Law and the Speed of Change

At some point, you've probably come across Moore's Law. Maybe you haven't heard it called that, but you're familiar with the concept developed by Gordon E. Moore, who in 1965 predicted that the semiconductor industry would be able to double the number of transistors on an integrated circuit every two years. That prediction has come true, and it now guides Silicon Valley's production targets. Like clockwork, each new device that uses a chip is exponentially faster than its predecessors.

This "speed of change" is mind-boggling when you think about it. Imagine if rates of return on savings doubled every two years, and had done so consistently for over 40 years!

What's amazing, and a little frightening, is that Moore's Law appears to drive more than semiconductor development. Memory and camera pixels are also doubling every two years. Just about anything digital is "improving" at a pace that is increasingly difficult to keep up with. Think about the number of emails you get every day!

Yet, for the most part, this is controlled change. Technology companies know and plan for these improvements.

What about disruptive change? Change that comes seemingly from nowhere, upends the market and overnight reinvents the game?

The financial meltdown of 2007 was such a change, it could be argued. The shockwaves that ripped through the financial services industry were staggering. From Lehman Brothers to Countrywide, names and faces that we had come to know were gone, just like that.

Even credit unions became collateral damage. Lending dried up, special assessments due to corporate credit union liquidations came home to roost, and added regulations in the guise of "financial services reform" hit us like a ton of bricks.

Who had an inkling of what was to come in the spring of '07 when the Dow broke 13,000 for the first time in history?

Our lives would be so much easier if we could predict the future. But we can't. The best we can do is to prepare for change. To be nimble and smart, to anticipate that next big wave before it breaks. As Wayne Gretsky so famously said, to skate to where the puck is *going to be*, not where it has been.

But how do we do that?

We're convinced that it starts with building great organizations. Great organizations are ready for and anticipate change. They're positioned to take advantage of opportunities, prepared to weather storms, motivated and staffed to excel and exceed members' expectations.

Change Management = People Management

Of course, change is never easy for any organization. In fact, according to Ken Blanchard in his *Mastering the Art of Change*, up to 70 percent of change initiatives fail! But we're convinced that by following some basic principles, you can guide changes in your organization.

One of the reasons managing change is so hard is because it involves people, and managing people during a time of change is a lot like herding cats. It's darn hard to cut through all of the topsy-turvy emotions, fear and resistance that accompany change. That's why well-intentioned leaders often fail.

In her book *The Change Monster*, Jeanie Daniel Duck writes about the "*human* forces that fuel or foil corporate transformation and change."

We think Duck hits the nail on the head when she says: "When people—executives, in particular—start a change initiative, they believe they understand what will be involved. But, once they get into the process, they are always astonished at how muddled, painful, protracted, tiresome, complicated and energy-consuming creating change can be."

As we noted in our introduction, credit union executives often come up through the ranks of the operations side of the business. Yet, as Duck notes, "Too many executives focus solely on the operational aspects of change, but to implement new ways of working requires people to think and act differently. To be fully effective, changes must address the intellectual and emotional issues—the hearts and minds—as well as the machines and systems."

The key takeaway from Duck is this:

Change is a dynamic process, not a series of events.

Dynamics are subtle and much more difficult to manage than events. Acquiring another credit union in a merger is an event. The shifting mood of your employees and those of the merged institution is a dynamic. Behaviors, attitudes, ideas, relationships— they all impact your ability to smoothly make needed changes in your credit union. If you don't factor in these human dynamics, you'll be stymied in your attempts to move your credit union forward.

The Basic Principles of Change Management

Let's consider some basics, then. These aren't rocket science, but they aren't necessarily easy, either. We can almost guarantee that if you follow them, change will be *less* painful at your credit union.

1. **Clearly communicate why change is necessary**. It's amazing how many leaders fail to make the case for change. Your change communications should be proactive, anticipating how people will react and how you will respond to their concerns. *Fear of change* is a very real hurdle that must be overcome, so take pains to address the impact on jobs, office locations and organizational structure.

2. **Involve your employees.** Studies show that employees often resist change because they weren't involved in the process. Look for ways to foster collaboration and solicit feedback. Involve your employees in the process so they feel ownership and can contribute to the outcomes.

3. **Solicit the help of your credit union's change agents.** In every organization, there are individuals who are quick to adapt to change. Seek out these change agents and make them your ally. Your life will be so much easier, and you'll have a ready pool of future leaders to draw from for key positions.

4. **Monitor your progress and make adjustments.** Set up a process for regularly collecting data on how a change initiative is progressing. How is everyone adapting to the new systems, workflows and processes? Do adjustments need to be made?

5. **Understand that change is a journey, not a destination.** Does change ever stop? No, of course not. So why do so many organizations, once they've completed a major project, lean back and say, "Hope we don't have to go through that again!" Guess what? You need to start planning for the next one!

The Six Stages of Change

You've probably heard the old saying, "A journey of a thousand miles begins with a single step." Learn to recognize and anticipate the steps to change. Here are what we consider to be the six basic stages (and roadblocks) to change:

1. **The realization that there's gotta be a better way.** So often change is forced upon us because we weren't paying attention. Learning to anticipate—to not be reactionary—means taking a hard look at your organization and developing a sixth sense about when things aren't right. It also means developing good listening skills (more on that in Chapter 3). Stage 1, then, is recognizing that the status quo isn't where you want to be. You need to change.

2. **Planning your future.** Strategic planning sessions, member feedback, industry trends—these all provide a framework for determining when

change is needed. But in order to move forward, you need a plan of action. Make sure, as we discussed earlier, that you involve your key stakeholders, including your staff and board. From here on out, there will be lots of uncertainty, fears and turf protecting as the initiative unfolds. Communication is key, and so is making sure all of your top people are onboard. Alignment is critical!

3. **Implementation.** As the saying goes, "Plan your work, and work your plan." Now comes the tough part, execution. Be prepared for resistance and for staff to want to remain in their comfort zone. For every step forward, there may be two steps back. Remember, you have to change people's mindsets as well as how they work.

4. **Perseverance and tenacity.** You're well into implementation, and "change fatigue" starts to set in. There's still uncertainty as to how things will work out. You may have had setbacks. You may be exhausted. This is when many organizations simply throw in the towel and put change on hold. So take stock of the situation. Be open and honest with your staff and board. Acknowledge mistakes, ask for their help and then get back on track.

5. **The finish line is near.** All those plans, meetings and hard work are starting to pay off. You're

seeing changes in attitude, new synergies. Morale is picking up, members are noticing. Numbers are improving. Keep it up!

6. **Transformation and celebration.** Looking back on all that you've been through, you begin to realize that your team accomplished a lot! It's time to celebrate and acknowledge everyone's contribution to a successful transformation of your organization.

Adapt, Evolve or Risk Irrelevance

Last year (2013), KPMG put out a report on the future of banking called *Reshaping Banking in a Dynamic Business and Regulatory Climate*. In it, KPMG emphasized the importance of getting out of "survival mode" and embracing change, creating new strategies and focusing on the customer.

According to KPMG, "[T]he rapid, unpredictable, and profound change we are witnessing is structural—not cyclical." KPMG added, "The debate is not about the need for change, but what changes should be made."

> *"Banking leaders must choose to adapt and evolve, or risk irrelevance," the report concludes.*

Those words weren't meant just for bankers; they apply to credit unions, too!

KPMG outlines a number of areas where financial institutions need to change. We don't think you'll see anything new here. At the same time, how many of these items are on your list of things to do?

- Focusing on customers, not products
- Deriving value from data
- Mergers/acquisitions/alliances
- Technology
- Cyber security
- Capital—Regulatory compliance and a better balance sheet

There Is Nothing Permanent Except Change

With this book, we are trying to equip you to step out of survival mode, to become more innovative, creative and forward thinking. Quite simply, the future of our industry depends on it.

As the Greek philosopher Heraclitus said, "There is nothing permanent except change." Change is constant, it's here and we need to get used to it.

Dan's Keys to Success

Harvard Business School professor John Kotter is a highly respected expert on change. His eight-step change model is well worth studying. Here's a quick rundown:

1. **Establish a sense of urgency**—Help others see the need for change, and they will be convinced of the importance of acting immediately.

2. **Create a guiding coalition**—Assemble a group with enough power to lead change, and encourage the group to work as a team.

3. **Develop a change vision**—Create a vision for change and strategies for achieving it.

4. **Communicate the vision for buy-in**—Make sure everyone understands and accepts the vision and strategy.

5. **Empower broad-based action**—Remove obstacles that undermine the vision; encourage risk taking.

6. **Generate short-term wins**—Plan for achievements that can easily be made visible, follow through on them and reward those who were involved.

7. **Never let up**—Change policies that don't fit the vision, hire and promote employees who can implement the vision, and reinvigorate the process.

8. **Incorporate changes into the culture**—Demonstrate the connection between new behaviors and success; ensure leadership development and succession.

Anthony's Takeaways

All companies do well. Until they don't.

Most companies form around an idea. That idea solves a problem, and people will pay for that idea. But time marches on. That original idea slowly becomes less valuable, and so does the company.

But this rarely happens overnight. Usually, companies respond to sagging sales by tightening their belt. They work harder, faster. All the while, the ground under their very feet is growing less stable.

I've seen it over and over. Companies refuse to change until they see the hangman's noose. Once the noose is in sight, change agents spring to life. Issues that once paralyzed an organization are swept away in a desire to stay in business. Change, or go away.

Too many companies wait until pending doom to make big changes. They drag their feet until it might be too late.

What a waste.

Now, do me a favor. Take out two pieces of paper.

On one, sketch how your credit union would be designed if you were starting it from scratch. On the other, write down a list of things that you'd start doing/stop doing if pending doom were staring you in the eyes.

Now, look at the things on those sheets of paper.

What in the world are you waiting for?

CHAPTER TWO

Vision, Values and Culture

*"Vision without action is merely a dream.
Action without vision just passes the time.
Vision with action can change the world."*
– JOEL A. BARKER

ere's a story that we think is worth repeating: A credit union we know hired a new CEO. One of the first things he did was clear out a glass case full of old dusty trophies and plaques that had been there for years. This case was next to a room where staff gathered for meetings and events. You really couldn't get into the room without first walking past the case, but, as he observed one day, no one even glanced at it anymore.

So he put the credit union's vision statement and values in the case for all to see. He put in the mission and goals, and he collected items from around the credit union that demonstrated progress towards those goals.

No longer was the case a dusty testament to past accomplishments, long forgotten. Now it was a living reminder of who the credit was, whom it served and what it believed in. Now there was a reason to pay attention because its contents looked forward, showcasing the work that made the vision possible.

That small change got the staff talking. It reminded them of why they came to work each day, what their purpose was and what they needed to do to live the credit union's values.

If you have a trophy case at your credit union, you might take a peak and see what's in there. Chances are it's full of dusty old relics from the past. Maybe some spring cleaning is in order.

The Vision Thing

Most of us are old enough to remember a certain president who spoke exasperatingly of "the vision thing." He got into a bit of trouble for that. His comments were indicative, though, of the attitude that many leaders have toward the corporate vision statement. They find it tedious and would rather just "make things happen."

As a consequence, vision gets delegated to outside consultants, who cobble together some lofty words after a boring all-day retreat.

What a shame, when the vision is really the essence of your organization. It's your enduring purpose, your corporate identity, the building block for your brand.

A few years back, NAFCU had Jim Collins speak at its Annual Conference. It was a real coup for us because he doesn't speak at very many industry events. We even had to go through an interview process to be accepted.

Boy was it worth it. Collins is a phenomenal speaker with an inspiring message about what it takes to take your organization from "good to great."

Collins and his team have done tons of research on what makes great leaders and how they build companies to last.

Guess what these companies have?

Yeah, a vision statement. And that's not all, but we'll get to that in a minute.

After they wrote their best-selling book *Built to Last: Successful Habits of Visionary Companies*, Collins and co-author Jerry I. Porras wrote an article for the *Harvard Business Review* called "Building Your

Company's Vision" that ought to be required reading at your next retreat.

"Companies that enjoy enduring success have core values and a core purpose that remain fixed while their business strategies and practices endlessly adapt to a changing world," they wrote. The companies they studied for their book, the ones with vision and an enduring core purpose, outperformed the general stock market by a factor of 12 since 1925.

Not a bad track record for "the vision thing."

In Chapter 1, we talked about how great organizations are able to navigate change. There is a key distinction to be made between blindly reacting to change and leading change.

As Collins and Porras note, "Truly great companies understand the difference between what should never change and what should be open for change... This rare ability to manage continuity and change—requiring a consciously practiced discipline—is closely linked to the ability to develop a vision. Vision provides guidance about what core to preserve and what future to stimulate progress toward."

The Two Parts to Vision

According to Collins and Porras, a well-conceived vision consists of two parts: **core ideology** and

envisioned future. Core ideology defines what an organization stands for and why it exists. The envisioned future is what the organization aspires to become, achieve or create.

Core values are those enduring tenets that have intrinsic value inside the organization. They are the heart and soul of the organization, and they are held independent of outside, external forces. They shouldn't be confused with operating practices or business strategies, which are subject to change.

We have talked to many credit unions that have developed core values, and we've been pleased to hear how these principles have been incorporated into the fabric of their organization.

If you haven't given thought to this, it isn't rocket science, as we like to say. It's best to keep your values simple, so they are easy to understand and repeat. Credit unions with winning cultures tend to emphasize three areas: serving the member, growing the business and developing employees.

Here are general categories where we typically see core values come from:

- Member service
- Financial strength
- Growth

- Community service
- Integrity, honesty
- Quality
- Employee investment

Putting your core values in public places in your headquarters and branches, placing them on your website—these are all simple ways of reminding and reinforcing what your credit union means to you and your members. But bear in mind that culture is not created by words plastered on walls or carried on laminated cards. Rather, it is defined by the actions you take. In a winning culture, words and actions are aligned. In a losing culture, they are misaligned.

Your Core Purpose

The "core purpose," what many simply refer to as the vision, Collins suggests, is not a goal or a business strategy. Rather, "it is like a guiding star on the horizon—forever pursued but never reached." Your core purpose, unlike a goal, may not be achievable; yet, it inspires change and stimulates progress.

Many organizations make the mistake of describing their business as their vision or purpose. For example, this is not a good vision: "We provide our members with convenient financial products and services."

The better vision statements we've seen for credit unions aspire to make a difference in members' lives and their communities, not provide products or services.

Visions don't have to be complicated. Wal-Mart's says, "We save people money so they can live better." Hilton's is "to fill the earth with the light and warmth of hospitality." American Express: "To be the world's most respected service brand." CVS: "To improve the quality of human life."

Having a vision and core values takes you one step closer to reaching your goals. It also becomes the touchstone for instilling the kind of culture you want your credit union to live and breathe.

Culture and Brand

It's been our experience that winning organizations pay attention to culture. We know that some credit unions have borrowed from the Zappos Culture Book model to create a document that describes, in the employees' own words and photos, what the credit union means to them.

Zappos CEO Tony Hsieh has said that "if you get the culture right, most of the other stuff—like great customer service, or building a great long-term brand, or passionate employees and customers—will happen naturally on its own."

We agree. The credit unions that are growing and "getting things right" are the ones with a strong sense of culture that translates into a compelling brand. The two definitely go hand-in-hand.

If employees have a clear sense of their credit union's "story," they will believe it and internalize it. Then the magic begins because they will *externalize* the culture and brand in their interactions with members and the public.

Employees and members can tell right away if your values are merely window dressing. It's the real deal when your employees want to come to work each day, and your members unequivocally rave about *their* credit union.

When you start hearing employees talk about your organization's core values in meetings and using them to guide important decisions, you know you're on to something.

Reinforcing Culture

While culture is intrinsic, something you can't just make up, there are ways to cultivate and reinforce the behaviors you and your team have decided best represent your organization. Here are a few ideas:

1. **Perform a culture audit.** Take a hard look at your organization to see if it is living its brand.

Talk to employees; review your vision and value statements. What's working? What's missing?

2. **Align your team.** You absolutely must have the right people on board. We'll talk about this more in Chapter 4.

3. **Use your core values to guide discussions and business decisions.** Your guiding principles should do just that: guide your actions. Encourage your teams to draw on your principles when discussing new projects and programs.

4. **Build core values into performance reviews and management systems.** Unless you reward people based on your core values, they will become empty words. Measure and reward behaviors consistent with your values. Weed out behavior that is not in alignment with your values.

5. **Reinforce values through communications, leadership development, training and retreats.** Like any behavior that you'd like to model or change, you must constantly reinforce your culture and in every way possible, including face-to-face training and retreats. Look for ways to create, teach, reinforce and reward on a continuing and enduring basis.

6. **Counter resistance with patience.** As we discussed in Chapter 1, change does not come easily. Expect some resistance, but counter it with examples of positive action based on your principles, and openly reward those behaviors that are consistent with your culture.

Winning Cultures Have Audacious Goals

Back in the 1960s, Americans were captivated by the notion of sending a man to the moon. From the time of John F. Kennedy's audacious challenge in 1961 to that historic day in 1969 when Neil Armstrong stepped onto the moon, NASA worked with passion and deliberation towards a single goal: sending a manned space expedition to the moon and safely returning it to Earth before the end of the decade.

NASA's goal is often cited as the classic example of a Big, Hairy, Audacious Goal (BHAG). We all need BHAGs to work towards, and organizations that have them are more likely to grow and succeed. They become the truly visionary organizations.

Remember at the outset, we said there are two parts to a vision: the core ideology and the envisioned future. This is the second part, the part that captures the imagination of the organization and propels it forward.

BHAGs are defined by Collins as being audacious (possibly not achievable), long-term (10 to 30 years) and capable of being vividly described. A true BHAG is clear, compelling and becomes a unifying focal point for teams to get behind. It engages people, it energizes them, and most important, it provides a finish line for them to shoot for.

BHAGs stretch you and your team beyond the strategic and tactical. They force you to be visionary as you grapple with where or what you want your organization to be 30 years from now.

We'll be talking more about goal setting in Chapter 7. But for now, be thinking about what might be a BHAG for your credit union.

Here's a BHAG for you to consider, courtesy of Collins: Which very large financial institution (though at the time a mere regional bank) had as its BHAG in 1915 "to become the most powerful, the most serviceable, the most far-reaching world financial institution that has ever been"?

If you guessed City Bank of New York (later Citicorp and now Citigroup), you're right.

Dan's Keys to Success

If you sat down with a cross-section of employees and members and asked them to describe the characteristics of your credit union, what would they say?

Hopefully you would hear good things. But that's beside the point. Whatever they say, good, bad or indifferent, they are defining your culture—at least how they perceive it.

So often we ask our members to rate us on what we do (how was the service?), but we don't ask them to rate us on who we are. It's not that difficult to improve service, extend branch hours or offer new products.

It's a lot harder to improve the intangibles—the values we stand for, the principles we aspire to. Yet, it is who we are that people judge us on—and remember long after they've left the branch or hung up from talking to the call center.

Now, suppose I asked that same cross-section of employees and members to describe your personal characteristics. What do you think they would say?

Let's hope they see reflected in you the same qualities they find appealing in the credit union. You and your credit union should be a mirror image. Why? Because you are the leader, and leaders are the standard-bearers for their organizations. They are the keepers of the culture, the chief advocates and architects, role models and boosters, all rolled into one.

Leadership by example is one of the most powerful ways to lead. When you exhibit the qualities you want your employees to aspire to, they will notice. Believe me, they will notice, and it will make a difference.

Anthony's Takeaways

You may be familiar with the work of Bain & Company. They're known for their periodic surveys of CEOs on management issues.

In their more recent work, which they wrote about last year (2013) on the *Harvard Business Review* blog, they focused on the connection between culture and performance.

Here are seven attributes of winning cultures from Bain & Company that are tailor-made for credit unions:

1. **Honest.** There is high integrity in all interactions, with employees, customers, suppliers and other stakeholders.

2. **Performance-focused.** Rewards, development and other talent-management practices are in sync with the underlying drivers of performance.

3. **Accountable and owner-like.** Roles, responsibilities and authority all reinforce ownership over work and results.

4. **Collaborative.** The best ideas come from the exchange and sharing of ideas between individuals and teams.

5. **Agile and adaptive.** The organization is able to turn on a dime when necessary and adapt to changes.

6. **Innovative.** Employees push the envelope in terms of new ways of thinking.

7. **Oriented toward winning.** There is strong ambition focused on objective measures of success, either versus the competition or against some absolute standard of excellence.

CHAPTER THREE

Communication

*"Imagine a world where what you say
syncs up, not sinks down."*
– STAN SLAP

Have you ever played that listening game where you whisper a sentence to one person, who in turn whispers it to the next, until it goes all the way around a circle? What starts out as "Dan and Anthony are going to the store to buy milk and cheese" ends up as "Dan and Anthony are at the door, and they forgot their keys."

It can be a lot of fun, but it never fails to impress on participants the importance of good communication skills.

Effective communication is especially critical when leading teams. We spend 80 percent of our waking hours sending or receiving information. Yet we often stumble when it comes to getting our message across.

We say we are good listeners, but do we really hear what others are saying? We're all for clarity, but then we hem and haw. Our speaking skills are sometimes embarrassing; our writing is unpracticed. We may be out of touch with employees, isolated from our members.

Is it any wonder, then, that people say "huh?"

And yet, if you want to manage change, motivate people or create a vision, you need to be at the top of your communication game.

Authentic Leadership = Authentic Communication

The best leaders are the best communicators, but not necessarily the most polished communicators. There's a difference. You don't have to be a golden-throated orator to make your point. You just have to connect at a human level, in an authentic and convincing way.

Management expert and author John Spence describes honest communication as a top leadership imperative:

"The single most important thing that people look for in a leader they would willingly follow is someone who will tell them the truth, who exhibits unquestioned integrity, who is a living example of the values they espouse and speaks with candor and transparency."

In Chapter 2, when we talked about the importance of vision and core values, we noted that authenticity is essential. You cannot fake a vision. You cannot wave a magic wand and make your organization's culture change.

So often, those who have risen to the top feel the need to adopt a new persona. They try to become someone they really aren't, someone out of Central Casting or a jumble of attributes from all of those leadership books they've read.

Our advice: Be yourself!

The word "communicate" has its root in the Latin for "share," "participate" and "common." At the heart of communication is the act of sharing yourself, participating and making common what you possess. Those are very good things to remember when you are communicating. Interpersonal skills are key.

If you've ever taken a public speaking course, you may have run across some interesting statistics attributed to Dr. Albert Mehrabian, who was a professor at UCLA and studied verbal and nonverbal communication.

The good doctor discovered in his research on how attitudes and feelings are communicated that non-verbal expressions (body language) and the way words are spoken (tone of voice) are much more important than the words themselves. In fact, it breaks down like this:

Words – 7%

Voice – 38%

Nonverbal – 55%

Often it's not *what* you communicate but *how* you communicate that counts. How you telegraph your feelings, how empathetic you are towards your staff, how genuine you come across—all have bearing on how well you will be able to lead your organization.

You can't go wrong if you communicate honestly and unambiguously, and with integrity, feeling and a touch of humility.

Listen, Listen: Learn, Learn

The old saying, "There's a reason why God gave us two ears and only one mouth," has a lot of truth: You'll get further by listening first and talking later. Follow the simple formula of "Listen, listen: learn,

learn." As Peter Drucker said, "Listening (the first competence of leadership) is not a skill, it is a discipline. All you have to do is keep your mouth shut."

You might start with active listening, where you confirm what you've heard by repeating it back to the speaker in your own words. This ensures that both you and the speaker understand each other. Active listening also means that you pay attention to body language and look for nonverbal cues. According to Drucker, "The most important thing in communication is to hear what isn't being said."

A willingness to hear other points of view, ask for feedback and accept constructive criticism are all hallmarks of an authentic leader. Listening promotes learning. After all, you cannot lead from ignorance.

One of the most effective ways of learning is to practice Management By Walking Around (MBWA), a technique first used extensively at Hewlett-Packard. In the age of email and social media, MBWA has even greater value than when HP managers were encouraged to walk around and see what their engineers were up to.

When you practice MBWA, make sure you take a genuine interest in what your teams are working on. You will not learn anything new if you don't have the trust of your staff and they feel uncomfortable talking to you.

In short, get out of your office and take advantage of every opportunity to interact with employees, members and the public. Practice good, old-fashioned two-way communication.

Be Your Credit Union's Chief Visionary

One of the most important jobs of a leader is to articulate the organization's vision. You should be the ambassador for your credit union's vision wherever you go.

Steve Buchholz and Thomas Roth, authors of *Creating the High Performance Team*, said, "The mediocre leader tells. The good leader explains. The superior leader demonstrates. The great leader inspires."

That sounds like a tall order, and you may ask, "How can I possibly inspire an organization?" But you'd be surprised. People can do extraordinary things when they believe and have passion for their mission.

Remember in the previous chapter when we were defining the characteristics of a Big, Hairy, Audacious Goal (BHAG)? A key aspect, according to Collins, is that the BHAG must be capable of being vividly described. It is an *envisioned* future. Your job is to describe that future in a way that your organization can see it, feel it and even taste it. Paint a picture that's so vivid that your employees can't help but get excited about it.

Express it so simply that everyone can understand it and repeat it to your members. Make it so compelling that everyone will want to be on board.

What does success look like at your credit union? Is it having more members? Opening new branches? Stamping out financial illiteracy in an underserved area? Offering member business lending? Whatever it is, become the chief spokesperson for the dream. Empower your staff through the words you use to describe what it's like to scale the mountain. Before you know it, you'll be an inspiration for your team.

It's All About Relationships

What's the best way to communicate as a leader? What are the best channels to use? What about social media? Should I be tweeting? Should I start a blog?

The digital age has ushered in many exciting new ways to communicate; however, in your rush to tweet or post, don't lose sight of a key fundamental: relationships.

Communication is fundamentally a relationship-building activity. Forming and deepening relationships should always be your number one goal.

Our advice is to select the media that helps you build the most enduring relationships with your members, whether it's print, broadcast, online or mobile.

Competitive pressures will dictate in some cases your choice of media. So will the popularity of the platform. But you'll want to devise ways to measure their effectiveness in reaching and engaging your members.

We would encourage you to experiment with the various digital tools available. We both have found blogging to be tremendously rewarding and an excellent way to connect with members.

Dan's Keys to Success

A few years ago, *BusinessWeek* had an article on "The Great Communicators" and featured some tips from top business leaders and personalities. See how many of these you do.

Jack Welch (former CEO of General Electric)
Best communication asset: Simplicity.
Tip: Eliminate jargon.

Meg Whitman (CEO of Hewlett-Packard)
Best communication asset: Penchant for listening.
Tip: Seek feedback.

John Chambers (CEO of Cisco Systems)
Best communication asset: Preparedness.
Tip: Review and rehearse your presentation.

David Neeleman (former CEO of JetBlue Airways)
Best communication asset: Talent for storytelling.
Tip: Tell tales that inspire.

Howard Schultz (CEO of Starbucks)
Best communication asset: Passion.
Tip: Identify and share what you're passionate about.

Rudy Giuliani (former NYC mayor)
Best communication asset: Ability to make eye contact.
Tip: Spend 90% of the time looking at your audience.

Klaus Kleinfeld (CEO of Alcoa)
Best communication asset: Ability to reinvent.
Tip: Stay fresh, remain current.

Richard Branson (CEO of Virgin Group)
Best communication asset: Generosity with praise.
Tip: Lavish appropriate praise on employees, customers and colleagues.

Anthony's Takeaways

I've been blogging for over six years now—first as NAFCU's "Compliance Guy" and more recently on my management blog, *Musings from the CU Suite*. I especially enjoy the many connections I've made with NAFCU members.

Blogging isn't for everyone, but it's taught me a thing or two about communication that I think is worth sharing:

Write with clarity. Knowing that I am going to push the "publish" button after I've written a post—and that the whole world will be able to see it—makes me think twice. Before you send an email, take a minute to read it. Does it convey what you want to say? Will you be embarrassed to see it a week or month from now?

Welcome comments. As much as I like writing, I live for the feedback I get from readers. Communicating is a contact sport. Always seek to engage.

Respect your reader. My readers are busy managers and executives. In exchange for their time, I always strive to deliver concise, well-written, upbeat content. Honor your readers.

Be consistent. I post at the same times every week, and I try to stay on topic. Be consistent in your communications—across all channels, in every media and in every message.

Put yourself into your communication. Communication is about relating to others. Be willing to share something about yourself, to poke fun at your foibles and show humility. You'd be surprised how that opens up people.

CHAPTER FOUR

Attitude and Enthusiasm

"A positive attitude causes a chain reaction of positive thoughts, events and outcomes. It is a catalyst, and it sparks extraordinary results."
– WADE BOGGS

Suppose you had a chance to start a new division or organization. Whom would you invite to be on your team?

Building a "dream team" can be exhilarating, the stuff that legends are made of. If you're a sports fan, you might think back to the 1980 "Miracle on Ice" U.S. hockey team that won an Olympic gold medal, or maybe the Oakland A's with Reggie Jackson, Vida Blue and Catfish Hunter, or the Pittsburgh Steelers with Terry Bradshaw, Franco Harris, Lynn Swann and John Stallworth.

In the business world, Jack Welch at GE, Lee Iacocca at Chrysler, Steve Jobs at Apple and Herb Kelleher at Southwest all built teams that either dominated or changed their industries. Their companies were known for their winning cultures.

In our judgment, getting the right people on your team—hiring with attitude and enthusiasm—may very well be the single most important thing a leader can do. To borrow an oft-quoted hiring prescription from Jim Collins, "start by getting the right people on the bus, the wrong people off the bus, and the right people in the right seats."

In fact, Collins' research demonstrates that great companies begin with "who" first and tackle "what" second. That is, getting the right people in the right positions in your organization is more important than *where* you are driving the bus. Strategy and tactics come after you've recruited your dream team.

Hiring for Attitude

In Chapter 2, we looked at the importance of developing a vision, creating core values and reinforcing the culture you believe best supports your organization's value system.

Doesn't it make sense, then, to hire and develop a staff that aligns with your core values and vision? A staff that will live your brand? Of course it does. And yet, many organizations simply don't do it. There is a disconnect between hiring decisions and creating a positive, winning culture.

Why? We think it has a lot to do with America's credential-obsessed approach to hiring. Managers always seem to get caught up in finding the candidate with the best résumé—the most impressive list of accomplishments, the best technical expertise and the right schooling. They're concerned with "what" people can do, not "who" they are.

Don't get us wrong. We're not saying you should hire mediocre talent or someone who doesn't have a good résumé. The good news is that talent and a good attitude usually go hand-in-hand.

What we're saying is that hiring for attitude wins nearly every time.

Mark Murphy, author of *Hiring for Attitude*, tracked 20,000 new hires and discovered that whenever new hires failed, 89 percent of the time it was for attitudinal reasons and only 11 percent of the time it was for lack of skill. "The attitudinal deficits that doomed these failed hires included a lack of coachability, low levels of emotional intelligence, motivation and temperament," Murphy reports.

He urges employers to focus on whether a candidate is motivated to learn new skills, think innovatively, cope with failure, assimilate feedback and collaborate with teammates. As Herb Kelleher used to say at Southwest, "We can change skill levels through training, but we can't change attitude."

Murphy cites Southwest, Google, Apple and The Four Seasons as great companies that hire for attitude. "Their high-performing employees live their attitudes every day," he says, "and it's a big part of what makes these organizations so successful."

Finding the Best People for Your Team

So how do successful organizations find the best people for their teams?

Well-known business consultants Jackie and Kevin Freiberg, who wrote the best-selling book *NUTS!* about Herb Kelleher and Southwest, spend a considerable amount of time advising top companies about hiring practices. They suggest identifying the superstars in your industry and creating a profile of common attributes they possess—then using this profile as your hiring target.

Examples that Freibergs identify for Southwest:

- Fun
- Unselfishness

- Trust
- Whatever it takes

If you've done the hard work of creating a vision and core values, this will come quite easily. Your values will become the blueprint for hiring people with the right attitude. Other attributes that we hear talked about at credit unions include:

- Integrity
- Honesty
- Team player
- Coachable
- Loves to serve others
- Aptitude for learning new things
- Passionate about work
- Risk-taker

But how do you know if someone is "unselfish" or a "learner"? The Freibergs suggest asking these questions during a job interview:

- Tell me about the last time you "broke the rules" to serve a customer in need. (flexibility; judgment)

- Tell me how you recently used humor to diffuse a tense situation. (fun)

- Tell me about a time when you went beyond the call of duty to assist a coworker when you received no recognition or no credit. (unselfishness; teamwork)

- Give me an example of how you've worked with an extremely difficult coworker. How did you handle it? (adaptability)

- Tell me about a time when you made a serious mistake with a customer or a coworker. How did you reconcile it? (ability to admit mistakes)

- Tell me about the last time you tried something new or took on additional responsibility when there was no guarantee for success. (willingness to take risks)

The key point to remember is that you aren't just "filling a position." The great companies have rigorous hiring practices for a reason. They understand that their people are more than employees—they are ambassadors for their business. New hires shape the culture and brand, and determine its future.

Motivate and Sustain Your Teams

Hiring for attitude is only half the battle. We realize that. The other half is creating and sustaining a positive environment that breeds enthusiasm. Motivating your team through positive reinforcement, recognition and rewards are all keys to building successful teams.

In the coming chapters, we'll be talking about teamwork and collaboration. We'll talk about trust, accountability and taking initiative. These are all very important. There is nothing more corrosive, in our judgment, than a negative attitude. Negativity breeds negativity. It needs to be weeded out and swiftly eliminated before it destroys your culture.

Back in the 1950s and 60s, psychologist Fredrick Herzberg asked a simple question: What do people want from their job? He set out to understand what motivates people to do a good job and what factors cause job dissatisfaction. The two-stage theory of employee motivation he advanced is now referred to as Herzberg's Motivators and Hygiene Factors. You may have heard of them or used them in your credit union.

It's important to understand these factors because creating an environment that is receptive to change and growth is fundamental to the work that we will be describing in the coming chapters. Take the time to assess your workplace. If there are motivational roadblocks, you'll need to remove them before you can start the important work of building highly effective teams.

Herzberg found that certain characteristics are consistently related to job satisfaction, while different factors are associated with job dissatisfaction. Here is how these characteristics get assigned by Herzberg:

Factors for Satisfaction	**Factors for Dissatisfaction**
Achievement	Company policies
Recognition	Supervision
The work itself	Relationship with supervisor and peers
Responsibility	Work conditions
Advancement	Salary
Growth	Status
	Security

What Herzberg found was telling: Satisfaction and dissatisfaction factors aren't related. They operate separately. Providing more factors of satisfaction, without addressing the factors of dissatisfaction, does not lead to greater satisfaction. Nor will simply eliminating dissatisfying factors lead to satisfaction.

In other words, eliminating dissatisfying job factors may placate your workers, but it will not improve performance. If you want to motivate your team, you need to focus on satisfaction factors like achievement, recognition and growth.

So really, there are two steps to improving your workplace environment:

Step One: Eliminate the causes of job dissatisfaction. These might include changing or eliminating outdated company policies, improving supervisory skills and organizational reporting structures, creating a culture of respect and dignity for all employees, providing job security and ensuring that your wages are competitive.

Step Two: Create the conditions that lead to high job satisfaction. Some obvious steps would be to provide opportunities for achievement, recognize outstanding work, create jobs that are rewarding, empower team members by giving them more responsibility, provide opportunities for advancement, and offer training and development.

You'll find that as you focus on eliminating the negatives and promoting the positives, your employees will respond in kind.

The Power of Positive Thinking

Never underestimate the power of positive thinking. As we noted in Chapter 3, the CEO's job is to embody in word and deed what the organization stands for. Ignite your organization with a purpose and passion that spreads like wildfire.

Here are a few tips:

Fuel others through "positivity." Tony Schwartz, president and chief executive officer of The Energy Project, likes to say that the CEO is the Chief Energy Officer. He writes in a *Harvard Business Review* blog post, "The way you're feeling at any given moment profoundly influences how the people who work for you feel. How they're feeling, in turn, profoundly influences how well they perform. A leader's responsibility is not to do the work of those they lead, but rather to fuel them in every possible way to bring the best of themselves to their jobs every day."

Beware of "SALLY." Sally isn't so much a person as it is a state of mind: **S**ame **A**s **L**ast **Y**ear. Sure, every organization does things on a regular schedule and follows a certain rhythm during the year. But that consistency can also breed complacency, to the point that things are always done the same way year after year. Our advice is to take a hard look at your SALLY events and see if you can blow one up. That is, simply start anew and see if the new version isn't better.

Continuous quality improvement. Instituting a CQI program means encouraging your teams to ask this basic question at the end of every project: "How can we do this better?" If you have a healthy CQI philosophy, you probably will have fewer SALLYs in your organization.

Extreme member service. At NAFCU, we're building a winning culture by emphasizing Extreme Member Service. EMS is a mantra that we all can get behind, and it extends to members we serve daily as well as our fellow staff. Delighting members becomes infectious and frankly second nature when you've hired and placed the right people into your organization.

Practice. "Practice isn't the thing you do when you're good," says Malcolm Gladwell. "It's the thing you do that makes you good." Remember that having a positive attitude is a habit, and habits need to be practiced every day in order to take hold. To borrow from the late Richard Carlson, author of *Don't Sweat the Small Stuff...and It's All Small Stuff*, "You are what you practice most."

Dan's Keys to Success

The late Steve Jobs said that he hired people for their passion. He looked for people who "wanted to put a dent in the universe."

How about you?

Is passion at the top of your list of hiring criteria? If it isn't, here are some reasons why it should be:

Passionate people are more creative. Drawing on 35 years of research into what motivates creativity, Harvard Business School professor Teresa Amabile and psychologist Steve Kramer reported in the *Harvard Business Review* that people "are more creative when they are more strongly intrinsically motivated—driven by interest, enjoyment, satisfaction and a sense of personal challenge in the work they are doing."

Passion is what drives performance. Without passion, Amabile and Kramer said, no amount of talent will yield great performance. "If you don't look for passion in the people you hire, you could end up with employees who never engage deeply enough to dazzle you with their creative productivity," they wrote. Ask people *why* they do what they do, not so much how they do it.

Passionate people are willing to do what it takes to become the best. Passionate people learn and improve so that their talent and contributions grow over time. Malcolm Gladwell suggests in his book *Outliers* that it takes 10,000 hours of practice to become expert enough to create an innovative breakthrough. Only passion can fuel that kind of persistence!

Anthony's Takeaways

How do the truly great companies find great people? What's their secret?

Peter Carbonara, writing for *Fast Company* a few years ago, decided to find out by following the recruiting teams at legendary companies like Southwest. Here are four rules he discovered for "hiring smart" that I think are worth passing along:

1. **What you know changes, but who you are doesn't.** "The most common—and fatal—hiring mistake is to find someone with the right skills but the wrong mindset and hire them on the theory, 'We can change 'em.'"

2. **You can't find what you're not looking for.** "The best way to select people who'll thrive in your company is to identify the personal characteristics of people who are already thriving and hire people just like them."

3. **The best way to evaluate people is to watch them work.** Great companies, Carbonara reports, aren't afraid to ask job candidates to role-play or "try out" in simulated job situations. They go to extraordinary lengths to hire the right person. Why? Because, as one executive said, "We can't afford to make bad hiring decisions."

4. **You can't hire people who don't apply.** "Companies that take hiring seriously also take recruiting seriously. Successful companies seldom lack for job candidates." A common tactic at successful companies: Rely on your existing team for referrals. Your top employees are likely your best source for new hires.

CHAPTER FIVE

Teamwork and Collaboration

"Unity is strength…when there is teamwork and collaboration, wonderful things can be achieved."
– MATTIE STEPANEK

I f you had to name your credit union's single greatest accomplishment, what would it be?

Introducing a new product or service? Adding to your field of membership? Opening a new branch?

Whatever it is, do you think it could have happened without teamwork?

No, of course not.

John Maxwell reminds us in his *17 Indisputable Laws of Teamwork*, "Nothing great is ever accomplished without teamwork."

When we think about the greatest teams ever assembled in business and research, we can't help but marvel at the heights they were able to reach, the breakthroughs they achieved and the innovations they ushered in.

Edison's Menlo Park, AT&T's Bell Labs, Lockheed's Skunk Works, Apple's Texaco Towers—hallowed ground in the annals of business history. The phonograph, light bulb, transistor, laser, U-2 spy plane and Mac—they were all built by teams, working together with a single purpose to reach a shared goal.

Your teams may not consist of Nobel Prize-winning scientists or world-famous inventors, but the members of those fabled teams of yesteryear put their pants on one leg at a time. They were human—no different than you or your employees.

On Any Given Sunday. . .

As former football commissioner Burt Bell famously said, "On any given Sunday, any team in the NFL can beat another team." That's generally true for any sport and in any endeavor in life.

It all boils down to teamwork and leadership. Those are the two winning ingredients. Talent? Sure, talent matters, but talent alone can never win games.

Indulge us for a moment, and we'll show you what we mean. We're going back in time to the first-ever industrial research laboratory, founded by Thomas Edison in 1876 in Menlo Park, N.J. Over 400 patents came out of the "Invention Factory."

What do we see if we peek in the windows? According to historians, Edison was the first to do the things that we now recognize as keys to creating breakthrough teams. For one thing, he assembled a group of people to help him invent. Until Edison came along, most inventors worked alone. Edison understood the value of collaboration. He also wasn't afraid to fail—many times, in fact—before finally succeeding.

As far as talent, Edison only had three months of formal schooling and was described as being "addled" by his teacher. Yet, he was later hailed as a genius for all of his inventions.

How did he do it?

The True Genius of Edison

Here is what we think is the true genius of Edison:

1. His teams were from different nationalities and different disciplines—a Swiss clockmaker, a British machinist, a German glassblower, an American mathematician—brought together to

work collectively on problems and to fashion workable solutions from his often half-formed visions. Edison thrived on their differences, instinctively knew how to draw out their strengths without favoring one approach or breeding like-minded "groupthink."

Lesson: Cultivate diversity, leverage strengths, welcome differing opinions and approaches to problems. Avoid groupthink that stifles creativity.

2. Menlo Park was called the Invention Factory in part because teams were working on multiple inventions at the same time. Progress or breakthroughs in one area could easily be transferred to another. Productivity could be accelerated. Edison gave his employees a goal to work towards, but he also gave them the freedom to be creative, to experiment and problem-solve.

Lesson: Give teams goals to strive for, then step back and let them work on a solution. Encourage sharing and experimentation.

3. Edison had a knack for inspiring his teams. He was most certainly a visionary leader, but he was also known for his "shoulder-to-shoulder" leadership. He visited his employees in the workshop, got involved in their projects, rolled up his sleeves and got just as dirty as they did. He inspired others by modeling the behaviors he

wanted to see in his teams and grooming his assistants to lead in the same way.

Lesson: Great teams have great leaders spurring them on, but they also learn from their leaders to self-manage, to inspire and motivate each other.

4. At least 20 inventors had tried unsuccessfully to electrify a light bulb before Edison. Those inventors worked alone and didn't share their ideas. Edison realized that if you put 10 people to work on a problem, you might just get a breakthrough. He also understood that human interaction was as important as technical know-how.

Lesson: Collaboration is as much about building relationships and trust as it is about creating innovative ideas. Collaboration occurs when teams value each other's contributions and work cooperatively towards a mutual goal.

5. Within a decade, Menlo Park had expanded to occupy two city blocks. Edison said he wanted his lab to have "a stock of almost every conceivable material." In short, every substance you could think of was available for experimentation.

Lesson: Make sure your teams have the resources they need to do their job.

6. Edison never gave up, quipping that genius is "1 percent inspiration and 99 percent perspiration."

He was convinced an electric light bulb was possible and drove his team to find a solution.

Lesson: Winning teams are driven to success by a passionate leader. They are the ones who are willing to "do whatever it takes" to make their dreams a reality. On any given Sunday...they come up with a win.

Dysfunctional vs. High-performing Teams

Some years ago, Patrick Lencioni, the best-selling business author, spoke at the NAFCU CEOs and Senior Executives Conference. Lencioni is probably best known for his *Five Dysfunctions of a Team*.

As you consider these five signs of dysfunction, think about the Menlo Park model. Also, think about your own teams. Do you see areas where you can improve?

Dysfunction #1: Absence of Trust
Fear of being vulnerable with team members prevents the building of trust on a team.

Dysfunction #2: Fear of Conflict
The desire to preserve artificial harmony stifles the occurrence of productive ideological conflict.

Dysfunction #3: Lack of Commitment

The lack of clarity or buy-in prevents team members from making decisions they will stick to.

Dysfunction #4: Avoidance of Accountability

The need to avoid interpersonal discomfort prevents team members from holding one another accountable.

Dysfunction #5: Inattention to Results

The pursuit of individual goals and personal status erodes the focus on collective results.

According to Lencioni, teams that are willing to address these five dysfunctions can become high-performing, cohesive teams. These highly effective teams:

- Avoid wasting time talking about the wrong issues and revisiting the same topics over and over again because of lack of buy-in.

- Make higher quality decisions and accomplish more in less time and with fewer resources.

- Are comfortable asking for help, admitting mistakes and limitations, and offering constructive feedback.

- Tap into one another's skills and experiences.

- Put critical topics on the table and have lively meetings.

- Align the team around common objectives.

- Retain star employees.

"No Man Is an Island..."

The most successful people understand that only by cooperating, collaborating and sharing can we do our best work and accomplish the most.

Think about Edison. Over his lifetime, he received nearly 1,100 patents! Do you really think he could have done that by himself?

John Maxwell says that even though people should know better, they still try to do things by themselves—usually for one of four reasons: ego, insecurity, naïveté or temperament.

So be on the lookout for these "reasons" for people electing to go it alone. Help them see the wisdom of teamwork. Remember the Bud Wilkinson quote, "If a team is to reach its potential, each player must be willing to subordinate his personal goals to the good of the team." This means focusing on the big picture so that you can work on the team's goals rather than your own.

Put another way, if you take the time to develop highly effective teams, your job becomes much easier. As Maxwell points out, where there is low morale, the leader must do everything; where there is high morale, the leader need only do little things. Be a high-morale team!

Dan's Keys to Success

An estimated 70 percent of U.S. workers are involved in some form of face-to-face teamwork. Over 40 percent are on virtual teams, with that number expected to rise to 56 percent in just a few years.

Older workers may not be comfortable with a team approach, but Millennial workers absolutely thrive on it. And by 2025, Gen Y will dominate the U.S. workforce with a population of nearly 80 million.

Millennial Inc. recently did a study on what a Millennial company of the future will look like. Not surprisingly, it will be a collaboratively led enterprise. Here are some key points to think about:

Flattened leadership. Millennials view success as something shared across the organization. Researchers asked Millennials to create a virtual company to see how they would structure it. Rather than assign a CEO, Millennials had each member focus on an area of responsibility.

Shared responsibility. While Millennials found it important to have areas of expertise, they all wanted to weigh in on other areas of the company. Eighty-two percent of those surveyed for the research said it is important to have staff that can do each other's jobs.

Decision by consensus. Millennials see value in bringing diverse thinkers together to make a decision. Fifty-four percent prefer to make decisions by consensus, and that number rises to 70 percent when they are among their peers.

Start polishing your team-building skills!

Anthony's Takeaways

Directors and officers have a legal "duty of loyalty" to their credit union, which means they "must act without personal economic conflict." To make "a self-interested transaction" is a breach of loyalty.

Unfortunately, the duty of loyalty sometimes gets lost in discussions of case law and litigation. That's too bad because there's a powerfully simple concept at work when you're loyal to an organization. It means putting your members first, removing "you" from your thoughts, and checking your personal biases, dislikes and baggage at the door.

To be truly loyal, you need to:

- Listen to dissenting views.
- Approach decisions with no preconceived notions.
- Listen more than you speak.
- Ignore rank.
- Tackle tough problems.
- Check your ego.
- Be respectful to colleagues.
- Be self-reflective.

During your career, I bet you've come across people that would do anything for the team. They give up their time at the drop of the hat. It is never about them. It is always about the team or the credit union. They are selfless. They are servants.

They are loyal. And to me, that might be the highest compliment possible.

CHAPTER SIX

Trust

*"The best way to learn if you can trust somebody
is to trust them."*
– Ernest Hemingway

With the possible exception of "love," is there any word in the English language as complicated as "trust"?

"Trust me."

"It's not that we don't trust you, it's just that…"

"Trust issues" extend from personal relationships to families and outward to businesses, organizations and national politics. Politicians' careers depend on it. Leaders can't lead without it. Parents can't parent if they don't have it. Couples can't survive if it's missing.

Yet, it's a lot like love. It's nearly impossible to explain, but we know it when we see it. We know it is an essential ingredient of leadership and that the loss or diminution of it has powerful consequences.

Stephen M.R. Covey, the author of *The Speed of Trust*, says that for many, "trust is intangible, ethereal, unquantifiable. If it remains that way, then people don't know how to get their arms around it or how to improve it. But the fact is, the costs of low trust are very real, they are quantifiable, and they are staggering."

Trust Has Real Impact

Covey suggests that low trust places a hidden "tax" on every interaction, decision or strategy, slowing organizations down and driving up costs. "My experience is that significant distrust doubles the cost of doing business and triples the time it takes to get things done," he says.

On the other hand, high-trust organizations earn a "dividend," Covey says, that is like a multiplier, enabling them to succeed in their communications, interactions and decisions and to move with incredible speed. He quotes a Watson Wyatt study showing that high-trust companies outperform low-trust companies by nearly 300 percent.

Ken Blanchard states that "productivity, income and profits are positively or negatively impacted depending on the level of trust in the work environment. Trust can be created or destroyed through personal perceptions and behaviors."

Lack of trust can lead to low morale in an organization. In his work with more than 1,000 leaders, Blanchard found that 59 percent indicated that they had left an organization due to trust issues.

In low-trust environments, employees who stay do so mostly for the paycheck. Their relationship with their employer becomes purely transactional, not exactly the kind of attitude and teamwork we described in Chapters 4 and 5!

What are the signs of a low-trust workplace? Here are a few that Covey mentions that you should strive to eliminate:

Redundancy: Excessive hierarchy, layers of management and overlapping structures designed to ensure control.

Bureaucracy: Complex and cumbersome rules, regulations, policies and processes.

Politics: Office politics wastes an organization's time, money, talent and energy. It can poison your culture, sabotage initiatives and ruin relationships.

Disengagement: Gallup estimates that employee disengagement costs $250–$300 billion a year!

Turnover: Low-trust organizations have greater rates of turnover than the industry average.

Fraud: Dishonesty, sabotage, obstruction, deception—these are a huge cost for organizations, especially financial institutions.

According to Covey, high-trust organizations see tangible results in lowered costs and in their ability to get things done. Here are a few results that he cites:

Increased value: High-trust organizations outperform low-trust organizations in total return to members and shareholders.

Accelerated growth: Consumers buy more, refer more and stay longer with companies and organizations they trust. We certainly have seen that with credit unions (vs. banks)!

Enhanced innovation: Creativity and sustained innovation thrive in a culture of high trust.

Improved collaboration: High-trust organizations foster collaboration and teamwork.

Better execution: There is a strong correlation between higher levels of trust and higher levels of execution.

Heightened loyalty: High-trust organizations earn higher levels of loyalty from their employees, customers, members, distributors, suppliers and investors.

Inspiring Trust

As we've noted in previous chapters, a leader has many responsibilities, ranging from being the organization's chief visionary to building and motivating teams. You can add to the list "inspiring trust." In fact, inspiring trust is a "must-do" activity that never goes away.

We've looked at lot of trust models, and most have several elements in common. At their core is creating a culture of integrity and competency, the twin pillars of trust. One really cannot operate without the other.

Integrity is one of those values we talked about in Chapter 2. Honesty, respect, transparency, loyalty—these are all attributes of integrity. Leaders must have integrity and show it, but they also must be able to demonstrate a level of competency that engenders trust. Employees and members must "trust" that you can actually do what you say you will and that your talk isn't just empty promises.

Ken Blanchard has developed what he calls the "TrustWorks! ABCD Model" that drives home this point about integrity and competence. We like it because it's fairly easy to remember your ABCs (plus a D): **Able, Believable, Connected** and **Dependable**. Here's a bit more about each one:

1. **Able** to demonstrate competence. Do you know how to get the job done and produce results? Do you have the skills to make things happen?

2. **Believable** means acting with integrity. Are you honest in your dealings with people? Are your policies fair? Do people feel they are treated equitably?

3. **Connected** is demonstrating care and concern for others. This means focusing on people and their needs, listening and openly sharing information about the organization and yourself.

4. **Dependable** is following through on what you say you're going to do. It means being accountable for your actions and being responsive to the needs of others.

Trust starts with that person you see in the mirror. Take a good look at yourself. If you don't possess integrity and competence, how can you expect to inspire it in others?

Trusting Others

The best leaders always lead with trust. They are inclined to trust, rather than to *not* trust. That seems counterintuitive to managers who have climbed the organizational ladder by minimizing risks and exercising tight control over projects and staff. But a funny thing happens when you trust others—they start to trust you. By giving up power, you actually create more. You empower teams to take risks, flourish and grow.

"When teams feel encouragement and support, rather than fear of retribution or embarrassment, they tend to take the kinds of risks that can lead to breakthroughs," says JetBlue Airways Chairman Joel Peterson. "Empowered workers can sense they are trusted. For most people, the feeling of being trusted leads to an increased desire to be trustworthy. This virtuous cycle can take your team to great interdependent heights."

The surest way to stifle creativity and risk-taking is to not trust your people, smother them in rules and foster a suspicious atmosphere that kills initiative. Here are five tips for fostering trust, taken from a very good series of LinkedIn blogs that Peterson wrote:

1. **Bet on people.** "Allow people *a chance to prove* they can take on more responsibility. A leader who trusts others to grow—knowing they may stumble—exhibits a level of trust that generally inspires the best in people and can ignite sparks of trust in an otherwise mistrustful environment."

2. **Take action.** "[W]hen people are actually *doing* things, iterating and refining as they go, they tend to get the best results. Empowering teams to act means missteps are less expensive and people learn faster."

3. **Don't forget the past. Okay, now forget the past.** "Institutional knowledge and process can be a valuable source of wisdom, but it may also represent deeply entrenched inertia...High-trust organizations don't rely blindly on old rules. Instead, they trust their teams to figure out the new ones."

4. **Expect foul-ups.** "Part of trusting team members with power is understanding that even the best efforts can, and do, falter. When it happens, the team should examine the reasons for the misstep, distill some lessons and move forward with renewed vigor."

5. Avoid the paraphernalia of paranoia.
"Trust-poor enterprises often assuage their fear of disaster with policy manuals, compliance committees, overactive legal departments and even rewards for turning others in. These practices give rise to an anxious, worst-case mindset that can squelch confidence and creativity."

Dan's Keys to Success

I'm always reading lists of things leaders can do to improve. So here's my own list of 21 things you can do to build trust. Tape them on your computer monitor. Share them with your staff. Add your own.

1. Lead by example.
2. Make yourself accessible.
3. Listen, learn and solicit feedback.
4. Encourage your staff to discuss and share ideas.
5. Be honest and transparent.
6. Involve employees in decisions that affect them.
7. Respect minority or unpopular views.
8. Right wrongs.
9. Do not blame others.
10. Spend time getting to know people.
11. Coach and offer opportunities for mentoring.
12. Don't micromanage—supervise without surveillance.
13. Avoid favoritism.
14. Create a respectful work environment.
15. Keep your promises and follow through.
16. Give second chances.
17. Constantly reevaluate.
18. Hold people accountable.
19. Commit to getting better.
20. Praise a job well done.
21. Have fun.

Anthony's Takeaways

"R-E-S-P-E-C-T."

"Just a little bit, just a little bit . . ."

You know the Aretha Franklin song. A hit in the '60s, "Respect" quickly became an anthem for the civil rights and feminist movements.

Respect also is the hallmark of high-trust organizations. In fact, Joel Peterson calls respect "the currency of trust." He writes, "You'll know you've got a high-trust organization when you find leaders showing respect to people at every level, especially those from whom they stand to gain the least."

Peterson urges leaders to root out disrespect and stay positive. That means zero tolerance for gossiping, talking behind people's backs, letting problems fester or failing to give people the feedback they need to improve. It means respecting others' opinions and recognizing that disagreement is often the key to great decision-making. In short, it's honoring people for who they are, not where they sit on the organizational chart.

How's your credit union doing with respect?

How tolerant are you of others' ideas or suggestions? How open are you to other viewpoints? If the answer is "just a little bit," you may have some work to do.

One way to show that you're serious about respect is to add it to your list of core values. But make sure you are paying more than just lip service to respect and that you make clear to your staff that *dis*respect has no place in your organization.

CHAPTER SEVEN

Accountability

*"It is wrong and immoral to seek to escape
the consequences of one's acts."*
– Mahatma Gandhi

Former President Ronald Reagan had a gift for communicating. One of the expressions he was known for was "trust, but verify." The story behind that saying is interesting because it is taken from a Russian rhyme, "Doveryai, no proveryai."

An expert on Russia taught Reagan the phrase for his meetings with the Soviets, explaining that the Russians like to speak in proverbs. It became his signature talking point leading up to the signing of the INF Treaty in 1987. Mikhail Gorbachev was reported to have said to Reagan, "You repeat that at every meeting." Reagan responded, "I like it."

We like it, too, because it reminds us that with trust comes accountability. Often in management books you see the two tied together, but we decided to treat them as separate chapters for a reason. We believe that trust always comes first, but too often leaders (and parents, teachers and coaches) condition their trust on expected outcomes and results.

The Russian proverb puts trust and verify in the right order. As we discussed in Chapter 6, leaders are always the first to extend trust. It's not easy putting yourself on the line, but extending trust while undermining it through actions that show that you really *don't* trust can cause more harm than good.

Accountability, like trust, starts with taking a look at yourself in the mirror. Leading by example means accepting the consequences of your actions and following through on promises. That not only builds trust, but it also shows your staff that you mean what you say and are willing to "own up" and hold yourself accountable.

JetBlue Chairman Joel Peterson says that trust is secured by accountability. Trust grows, he writes, "when expectations are clear, when people know what they've been empowered to do, and when they can focus on doing it." If you truly want your teams to perform at their peak and deliver extraordinary member service, then you must make clear what it is you want—and what the consequences are of not meeting those expectations.

Clarify the Task At Hand

So the first step in building a culture of accountability is to clarify the task at hand. Leaders have a responsibility to communicate their organization's vision in clear, easy-to-understand terms. As we discussed in Chapter 3, your job is to describe what winning looks like, right down to the last detail. This is not a pie-in-the-sky wish list. It's concrete, executable goals with timelines and expected results.

We've all been involved in a project or committee that doesn't have clear expectations. It's frustrating, isn't it? But when concrete goals are communicated, everyone breathes a sigh of relief. Finally, something we can sink our teeth into and accomplish!

Here's a little secret: High performers thrive on goals. They understand that being given responsibility is only half of empowerment. The other half is knowing exactly what you are being empowered to do! Without those expectations, even your best people will flounder, stuck in a gray world of vague objectives where no one is sure what success looks like.

Notes Peterson, "If you haven't spent much time in a high-trust environment, accountability may initially feel like *mis*trust. Some people might ask, 'Is it really trust if you're asked to constantly account for the power you've been granted?' The answer is yes. In order to survive and grow, organizational trust has to be protected from misuse. Without accountability, trust doesn't have a chance."

Set Measurable Goals

For all of their tough talk about holding people accountable, many managers and leaders aren't very good at it. One study done by Darren Overfield and Rob Kaiser, and reported in a *Harvard Business Review* blog post, found that "one out of every two managers is terrible at accountability." The two studied over 5,000 top-level managers in the U.S. and around the world and found that 46 percent had failed to hold their people accountable.

Let's face it, telling someone that they're not performing well is never a pleasant experience. It helps, though, when you have measurable goals in front of you—when it's clear to both you and your team members that they've fallen short. There's no ambiguity; it's right there in black and white. Those conversations are better because everyone starts with a given, and then you can move on to discuss what needs to improve.

The only way to have productive conversations like that is to first lay the groundwork for clear roles and responsibilities and measurable results.

If you're familiar with "SMART," you know that's a good place to start with goal-setting.

SMART is the acronym introduced in 1981 by George T. Doran in his *Management Review* article, "There's a S.M.A.R.T. Way to Write Management's Goals and Objectives." When you understand what SMART stands for, it's pretty easy to see how it applies to goal setting:

S – Specific
M – Measurable
A – Achievable
R – Realistic (or Relevant)
T – Time-bound

Committing to Improvement

Once you've gotten your SMART goals down, your management team can assign tasks accordingly, right? Well, not so fast. For accountability to work, you have to make a commitment to your teams that you will provide certain essentials. These are pretty self-evident, but they are worth mentioning. Here are a few taken from a list by Henry Browning, author of *Accountability: Taking Ownership of Your Responsibility*:

Support from you and your senior managers. Make it clear that you have your teams' back and firmly stand behind their goals.

Resources to do the job. Give your teams the budget and staffing they need to get the job done.

Access to information. Keep your teams in the loop. Make sure they have the data they need to make sound decisions.

Freedom. If there is too much direction from the top, team members will not take ownership. Empower them to decide how to accomplish a task.

Reward risk-taking and learning. Create a culture that rewards risk taking and treats mistakes as learning experiences.

One of the key points about accountability is that it's not about punishment. Rather, it's about improvement. Always keep that in mind. Here's what Browning has to say:

It's not about punishment. "If your goal in fostering accountability is to know who to punish when revenue targets are not met or budgets are missed, you will only succeed in creating fear. No one will be willing to step up, speak out or try something new. Innovation and risk taking will be lost."

It's about improvement. "Accountability is the foundation for creating a learning organization. If you want sustainable high-quality processes, you need to be able to see what's working and what isn't—and analyze the cause."

Evaluating and GROWing

In high-accountability cultures, everyone expects to be evaluated. No one flies under the radar. As Browning points out, people seek feedback "because they know it is intended to improve the process and add to their knowledge." If they fall short, they are the first to admit it and work to improve.

At the same time, very few fears are as strong and difficult to overcome as the fear of failure. How you treat the person who has failed, even the demeanor you use, will have a huge impact on that person and the rest of your organization.

So what do you do about those employees who aren't performing? The ones that just keep falling short?

Well, one thing you can do is talk to them. That's not rocket science, but as we've said, darn few bosses are good at it. Sometimes just talking through a problem leads to solutions. But it starts with finding out if there are circumstances contributing to the person's less-than-stellar work. Chances are something is at the root of the problem.

If you're looking for a good a blueprint for these kinds of discussions, we'll give you another acronym we like. It's called the GROW model and is often used in coaching and mentoring. You might try it out.

G – Goal

R – Reality

O – Options (or Obstacles)

W – Will (or Way Forward)

GROW starts with establishing or revisiting your goals and then assessing your current reality. Where are you with your goal, and what is stopping you from achieving it?

Next comes exploring your options and brainstorming possibilities. What else can you do to reach your goal? What obstacles stand in your way? What behaviors need to change?

Finally, you must commit or recommit to achieving the goal. You must figure out the way forward. Some of this motivational, so build in steps that lead to progress, but also make sure you are building in accountability.

Dan's Keys to Success

You've heard it many times, often after a team loses a game: "They just couldn't execute."

Failure to execute is one of the biggest reasons why organizations fail. It often is a sign that something more serious is going on—lack of leadership or vision, poor planning, or lack of investment in technology, people or infrastructure.

It's not enough to create a culture of accountability; make sure you're also building a culture of execution. Here are some ideas that I think will help:

- Assign individuals specific tasks with firm completion dates. Be clear about who does what and when it's due.

- Cut down on needless meetings; give your staff time to get their work done.

- Measure outcomes, not processes. Too many organizations measure the wrong things, without a clear sense of the desired outcomes.

- Reward people for results, not "busy work."

- Learn to prioritize. Don't take on too many projects at once, and keep ad hoc projects to a minimum.

- Show your team how goals, vision and strategy relate to their job. Make sure what's happening on your front line is aligned with your goals.

- Review execution frequently. Organizations that review monthly perform better than those that review quarterly. Those that review weekly do best.

Anthony's Takeaways

As leaders, we have a tendency to want to fix things. But what are we teaching our employees when we solve their problems for them?

Perhaps you've read the *Harvard Business Review* article, "Management Time: Who's Got the Monkey?" It's a classic from 1974 and has been reprinted many times. Written by William Oncken Jr. and Donald L. Wass, it describes a harried manager who has taken on too many "monkeys."

A monkey is a subordinate's problem that leaps onto your back the minute you offer to help. Pretty soon you're carrying everyone's monkeys on your back, and you don't have time for your own job. Managers need to return monkeys to their rightful owners and empower employees to handle their own problems.

In an afterword written with the help of Stephen R. Covey, the authors suggest ways to delegate and eliminate monkeys. Here are few you might consider:

1. Avoid discussing monkeys on an ad hoc basis. Schedule a brief appointment to discuss the issue.

2. Do not offer a solution. Instead, suggest that the employee recommend a course of action and then implement it with your approval; or the employee may take independent action and advise you of the results.

3. Agree on a status update.

4. Develop your employees' problem-solving skills and instill in them the confidence to tame their own monkeys.

CHAPTER EIGHT

Learning

*"Learning is not a product of schooling
but the lifelong attempt to acquire it."*
– ALBERT EINSTEIN

Job applicants these days like to describe themselves as life-long learners. Management experts brag about creating learning cultures and promoting continuous improvement. HR people talk about L&D (learning and development). At universities, "blended learning" has become the rage, with more and more course offerings on the Internet.

Never has learning been more important in developing a competitive workforce, equipped to innovate and lead in an increasingly complex and changing world.

Credit unions have long understood the value of learning, especially when it comes to training their front-line staff. Keeping tellers and member service representatives properly trained is one of the biggest challenges facing credit union managers. Keeping up with regulatory changes has become a full-time job as well.

But is training the same as learning?

It's one thing to brush up on your job skills or read about a new compliance requirement. That's the basic stuff of doing your job, right? But how do you create a culture that encourages risk taking, feedback and reflection? An environment where it's okay to try new things and learn from mistakes? A place where knowledge is shared and applied in innovative ways? A culture of inquiry where employees feel safe asking tough questions about how well you're serving members or what can be done differently to achieve better results?

Beyond Checking the Box

Too many organizations view learning as a "check-the-box" activity, with little thought given to its strategic value. Employees get onboarded and receive skills training. They attend classes and seminars, maybe even an in-house "leadership institute."

Those discrete doses of knowledge are important, but they don't seem to be part of a coherent whole.

Take a look at this comparison between training and learning, and you'll see what we're getting at:

Training	**Learning**
Doing	Understanding
Skills development	Behavior change
Short-term	Long-term
Meets current objectives	Prepares for future
Structured	Organic
Prepares for the "known"	Prepares for the "unknown"

While training is certainly vital to running an operation, it's but a part of what should be a continuous learning culture. Here are some questions to consider as you think about how to make learning and continuous improvement a key part of your credit union's core values. See how many of these you answer "yes" to:

1. Are we constantly learning how to improve performance?

2. Are we gathering feedback and acting on it?

3. Do we reward employees for taking the initiative to learn new things?

4. Are we constantly trying to learn how to have more effective meetings and events?

5. Are we constantly learning to improve processes, products and services?

6. Is experimentation and risk taking supported and not punished?

7. Do employees understand what they need to learn to help the organization be successful?

8. Are we coaching our employees to help them become better at their jobs and improve the organization?

9. Do employees receive frequent formal and informal feedback on their job performance?

10. Do teams and departments share what they have learned with each other?

'HILOs' Perform Better

If you answered "yes" to most of the above questions, congratulations! You may be a "high-impact learning organization" or HILO. A few years ago, Bersin & Associates published a research report on HILOs. The consulting company found that organizations with highly developed learning cultures significantly outperform their peers in many areas:

- They are 32 percent more likely to be first to market.

- They have 37 percent greater employee productivity.

- They have a 34 percent better response to customer needs.

- They have a 26 percent greater ability to deliver quality products.

- They are 58 percent more likely to have skills to meet future demand.

- They are 17 percent more likely to be a market-share leader.

That's pretty impressive!

How'd they do it? According to Bersin, HILOs made learning a part of their business strategy and incorporated it into performance management. They made belief in learning a part of their leadership development programs and encouraged managers to take ownership of the learning culture.

HILOs started the learning process early, using onboarding programs to encourage new employees to take personal responsibility for learning. Onboarding didn't end with new hires, though; it continued throughout an employee's career.

HILOs made work educational by using embedded learning techniques. They applied learning to real-life business problems and in a way that allowed employees to reflect on what they'd learned.

Finally, knowledge sharing was an organizational habit at HILOs, and coaching and development were a key part of the performance review process.

Creating a Learning Culture

Paul J.H. Schoemaker, a professor at Wharton and author of *Brilliant Mistakes: Finding Success on the Far Side of Failure*, has written about what it takes to create a positive learning culture. Here are some additional tips we've gleaned from his writings to help you on your path to becoming a HILO:

1. **Make learning a daily habit.** "As with sports, unless you practice a lot you will not get better. True learning organizations reward new patterns of thinking and reinforce the underlying skill sets."

2. **Set the example.** "Since 'learning from example' is contagious, the behavior of the boss becomes critical. Leaders should be the focal point as well as champions for learning. They are best positioned to shine a bright spotlight on success as well as failure, and see to it that mistakes become sources of new learning."

3. **Don't be defensive—confront failings honestly.** "A key imperative for learning from experience is the willingness to look squarely at one's own performance in a transparent and nondefensive manner. The U.S. Army institutionalized the practice of After Action Review to immediately learn from what went well and what did not work in a mission. After Action Review is a structured process for analyzing what happened, why it happened and how it can be done better the next time."

4. **Allow mistakes and celebrate them at times.** "Mistakes are valuable sources of learning, and leaders should intentionally allow mistakes in select situations to challenge deeply held assumptions. If your organization gives performance awards at key meetings, make sure to celebrate a few cases where the results were disappointing but the process followed was sound."

Everyone Needs to Learn... Especially Leaders

Schoemaker notes that "many organizations make learning an optional activity, one from which the senior team is far too often exempt." It does seem that those who have reached the senior ranks sometimes stop learning. They view learning as something for their employees but not for them.

Yet, great leaders are relentless in their pursuit of knowledge. Most are avid readers, devouring books at a prodigious pace. Bill Clinton, Oprah Winfrey and George W. Bush are a few that come to mind. Bush wrote in his memoirs that he and Karl Rove competed to see who could read the most history books in one year. He read 95, and Rove read 110.

The quest for knowledge is a discipline, a way of life, and a realization that we are not perfect and can always learn more. Michelangelo is said to have inscribed the words "ancora imparo" on the edge of a sketch at the age of 87. Loosely translated, it means, "I am still learning."

How about you, are you still learning?

If you need to rekindle your management team's passion for learning, you might borrow a page from Amazon CEO Jeff Bezos' playbook. Bezos asked his top executives to read three books and join him in a day-long "book club" discussion of each one, followed by dinner. Bezos said he used the books as frameworks for charting the future of Amazon. What were the three books? Drum roll…

The Effective Executive by Peter Drucker

The Innovator's Solution by Clayton Christensen

The Goal by Eliyahu Goldratt

You can bet those books are on a lot of nightstands right now!

We also like the concept of reverse mentoring, an idea championed by Jack Welch when he was CEO of General Electric. The idea has caught on at other companies, where senior executives are paired with younger employees to learn about social media, technology and emerging workplace trends. The older mentees are learning new skills, and the young mentors are getting access to top execs and an inside view of management.

And speaking of mentoring, here's an idea we first read about from Brenton Weyi, an entrepreneur and motivational writer. He suggests that to be successful, you need to have three "essential" people in your life at all times:

1. *"A person who is older and more successful than you to learn from."*

2. *"A person who is equal to you to exchange ideas with."*

3. *"A person below you to coach and keep you energized."*

He cites Aristotle as the perfect example of this principle. Aristotle learned from his mentor Plato, exchanged ideas with other Greek philosophers in the Academy and taught a young boy named Alexander. Hmm, could that be Alexander the Great?

Dan's Keys to Success

I'm a firm believer in learning by doing.

Don't get me wrong, I believe in formal education, too. After all, my father was a college professor, and I was fortunate to receive a master's degree from Harvard University. But it's important for organizations to understand that not everyone learns the same way.

What motivates me to learn may not be the same as what motivates you.

When my daughter was younger, I would go down in the basement and paint with her. I taught myself to use oils and an ink wash called sumi-e. I had a couple of art showings, even. For me it was a release, a way to spend time with my daughter and to think and see in a totally different way than I was used to.

I'm also an amateur fly fisherman. A couple of years ago, I entered a fly-fishing tournament. I probably learned more in that one weekend from talking and being around pros than I had in all the years I had been fishing on my own.

My point is that we learn in different ways. As leaders, we need to always be looking for new ways to see, learn and do. Take the time to talk to people, to master new skills and observe the world.

By the same token, understand that your staff needs to learn some by doing, some by talking to others, some by reading and studying, and some by coaching and mentoring. There is no single, best way to learn.

Anthony's Takeaways

If you're looking for a simple, foolproof formula for continuous improvement in your credit union, you can't go wrong by going to the source of quality control, Dr. W. Edwards Deming.

While Deming's work became the model for Japanese car manufacturers and their quality circles, his PDSA Cycle, or "wheel of continuous improvement," has been used by all types of organizations. Based on the scientific method, here's how it works:

1. **Plan**—Analyze the current situation, gather data and develop ways to make improvements. Ask yourself these three questions:

    a) *What are we trying to accomplish?*

    b) *What changes can we make that will result in improvement?*

    c) *How will we know that a change is an improvement?*

2. **Do**—Test the alternatives in a prototype or pilot program with a select group of members.

3. **Study**—Determine whether the pilot or trial worked as intended, whether revisions are needed or if it should be stopped.

4. **Act**—Implement the changes in your organization or with your members so that the improvement becomes standardized.

These four steps are repeated over and over as part of a never-ending cycle of continual improvement. It's that simple.

CHAPTER NINE

Time Management

*"Time is the scarcest resource, and unless
it is managed nothing else can be managed."*
– PETER DRUCKER

Do a Google search on "time management,"
and you'll get well over a billion results. Yes,
that's billion with a b. It may very well be the most-
written-about topic in the pantheon of popular business topics. It eclipses leadership, change management, teamwork, corporate responsibility, sustaina-
bility, technology and innovation.

So much has been written about time management,
productivity and getting things done, that it's hard
to know where to start. Even the phrase "Getting
Things Done" is registered by time-management
guru David Allen!

We've been saying all along that leadership and management ain't rocket science (although it isn't easy, either). That certainly goes for time management. Most of the methods and systems we've looked at aren't the stuff of doctoral dissertations. They're commonsense prescriptions that have proven effective over time. In fact, some of the most tried-and-true suggestions go back centuries.

Using Time Wisely

For example, we can thank Ben Franklin for phrases like "time is money" and "early to bed and early to rise makes a man healthy, wealthy and wise." These and other proverbs collected in *Poor Richard's Almanack* have distinctly shaped the American approach to time and its use.

We'll take a look at Franklin's daily routine in a moment, but one of the more noble things about it (which we have from his autobiography) is that he began each morning with a meditation on the question "What good will I do today?" And he ended the day by asking, "What good have I done?"

We bring this up because as leaders, our time is not our own. We have a responsibility to use our time wisely and for the good of our organization. Leaders serve as examples of time management for their teams.

Employees pay close attention to their bosses' comings and goings. They're mindful of when you arrive and when you leave; what your office and desk look like; whether you keep your door open; what's on your calendar; what you do for lunch; how you conduct meetings, delegate and follow up; and how quickly you make decisions and get things done.

If you're not happy with your organization's use of time, take a look at your own time-management habits and those of your managers. You might see that it's a simple case of "monkey see, monkey do." Be a time-management model for your employees; show them how they should be using their time.

Changing Habits

In many ways, time management boils down to changing habits and practicing old-fashioned virtues like discipline and self-improvement. This is why time management is included in so many motivational books. It takes a lot of willpower to stick to a schedule or force yourself to do those things you know you need to do.

Much of the same principles that we wrote about in previous chapters on attitude and accountability apply to personal time management. There really is no substitute for the mental energy, stamina and hard work it takes to start each day charged up and ready to go, and to stay on track and tackle the tough tasks that need to be done.

Generals, presidents, coaches and captains of industry have all been admired for their ability to get results. What's their secret? It turns out, they all have their own way of doing things. In a remarkable book by Mason Currey, *Daily Rituals: How Artists Work*, we discover that "there's no one way to get things done."

Currey studied the habits of hundreds of famous artists, writers, composers, architects and creative thinkers, only to find that some preferred to work in the morning while others were night owls. For nearly every rule of time management, Currey found celebrated exceptions.

However, Currey did find one thing in common among the highly successful people he studied: they had daily rituals.

Establish a Daily Routine

If we had only one piece of advice to give you, it would be to establish a daily routine. And that takes us back to Franklin, who most decidedly was a stickler when it came to his daily "Scheme." Franklin mapped out his day in hourly increments, although some were obviously lumped together, as in 10 p.m.–5 a.m. for sleep, and 8 a.m.–noon and 2–6 p.m. for work.

He rose at 5 a.m. to meditate ("Rise, wash and address Powerful Goodness!") and plan his day ("Contrive day's business, and take the resolution of the day; prosecute the present study, and breakfast"). The "present study" may have been one of 13 virtues or habits Franklin practiced on a daily basis for one week at a time and repeated four times a year.

Laura Vanderkam, author of the popular book, *What the Most Successful People Do Before Breakfast*, writes that "before the rest of the world is eating breakfast, the most successful people have already scored daily victories that are advancing them toward the lives they want."

Most CEOs, she reports, are up before 6 a.m. at the latest. They also have learned this one little lesson about life: "If it has to happen, then it has to be first." That is, first thing in the morning is the time to get things done, when you are fresh and have the time for reflection, exercise, reading and planning your day.

Peter Bregman, author of *18 Minutes*, suggests starting the day by making two lists, a "focus list" (the road ahead) and an "ignore list" (the distractions).

On your focus list, write down not only those things you need to accomplish but also what's important to you. Design your time around those things. On your ignore list, write down what you are willing to forego, what's not important. Learn to eliminate the distractions that keep you from focusing on the important things.

"Focus" and "ignore" questions should be asked anew each day, Bregman says. Review them every morning, along with your calendar and ask, "What's the plan for today?" Sounds a lot like Franklin, doesn't it?

Incidentally, Jim Collins has said that great business leaders know when to eliminate those things that aren't working. He is one of many business experts who suggest creating an annual "stop-doing" list.

"Eat That Frog"

Brian Tracy, author of *Eat That Frog*, recommends that you start your day "eating a frog." Eating a frog is his shorthand for tackling your most challenging tasks first, while you're still fresh and before you get busy with something else.

Getting your frogs out of the way paves the way for being more productive the rest of the day. It then gives you the time to take on other tasks and ensures that you won't end the day without having accomplished what's really important.

What are some of your frogs? If you're not sure, consider these three questions, and you'll probably have the answer:

1. *What are my highest-value projects and activities?*

2. *What can only I do (and no one else) that if done well will make a difference?*

3. *What is the most valuable use of my time right now?*

Think of it this way: Suppose you have a bucket you need to fill with rocks, pebbles and sand to carry to a construction site. To make the fewest trips possible, you put the big rocks in first, right? Then you can add pebbles and fill in sand. Plan for big issues first, or inevitably the pebbles and sand will fill up your days.

Along this same vein, Dwight D. Eisenhower famously divided tasks into four categories:

- Urgent-important items were dealt with immediately.

- Urgent-unimportant items were delegated.

- Not urgent-important items were entered into a calendar.

- Not urgent-unimportant items were minimized or eliminated.

The "Eisenhower box," as it's sometimes called, is the same four-quadrant time management model popularized in Stephen R. Covey's *The 7 Habits of Highly Successful People*.

Balance Your Workload

According to a recent survey by McKinsey & Company, most executives feel they are falling behind. McKinsey gives examples of executives so overloaded that they lack the capacity to lead crucial new programs. The proliferation of big strategic initiatives and special projects has led to "initiative overload," McKinsey says.

However, there is some hope. McKinsey found that the most "satisfied" executives (those who felt they were able to get things done) had achieved a balance in their work lives. These execs spent about a third of their time interacting with external stakeholders, 39 percent in internal meetings and another 24 percent working alone.

Satisfied managers divided their workday evenly among: making key business or operational decisions, managing and motivating people, setting direction and strategy, and managing external stakeholders. They also spent less time on administrative tasks.

More specifically, McKinsey gives these excellent tips for reducing overload:

1. **Have a "time leadership" budget—and a proper process for allocating it.** As McKinsey puts it, how much leadership capacity (time) does your organization really have to "finance" its great ideas? Treat human capital the same as financial capital.

2. **Think about time when you introduce organizational change.** That is, how much time is it really going to take to achieve the organization's goals?

3. **Ensure that individuals routinely measure and manage their time.** McKinsey discovered that while most executives can tell you how much of the budget is dedicated to their priorities, they don't know how much time is devoted to them. Time also gets misallocated when employees spend too much time on measurables that aren't aligned with strategic objectives. McKinsey recommends putting time-related metrics in managers' performance reviews to keep them focused on what matters most to the company.

4. **Refine the master calendar.** Not only should you keep a master calendar, but you should use

it to root out corporate time-wasting such as unnecessary meetings.

5. **Provide high-quality administrative support.** McKinsey found that effective time managers receive strong administrative support. The CEO, in particular, needs to have a capable admin who can "own" the master calendar and ensure that the executive team's time in meetings is devoted to the organization's priorities.

Eliminating Time-wasters

What are the biggest time-wasters in your organization? Too many (poorly run) meetings? Too many emails? Here are a few ideas we've collected for busting the time bandits in your organization:

Kill a stupid rule (and stupid meetings and reports). Eliminate what's holding you back. This comes courtesy of Lisa Bodell, CEO of Futurethink and author of *Kill the Company*, who was a keynote speaker at NAFCU's Strategic Growth Conference.

NNTR. When sending out informational emails, put NNTR (No Need to Respond) in the subject heading. It will cut down on needless email traffic. (Again, from Lisa Bodell.)

Turn off email notifications. Turn off those annoying email and IM notifications that flash across your screen or ping your smartphone. Establish a routine for when you read and respond to emails during the day.

Set limits on your time. Be firm and diplomatic in dealing with time allocated for meetings, paperwork, telephone and visitors. Establish blocks of time when you are available for visitors. Keep your meetings brief and agree to an ending time. (More on meetings in Dan's Keys to Success.)

Avoid small talk on phone calls and stand up. Try standing up while you're on the phone. It makes a difference! Not only does your voice change (you sound more confident), but you'll find yourself getting to the point quicker. Standing up works for meetings, too.

Handle mail, emails and inbox items only once. This is an old rule, but we all violate it from time to time. Try not to touch anything more than once. If you take it out of your inbox, don't put it back.

Avoid multi-tasking. Yes, it's true, we humans weren't designed to do more than one thing at a time. Research shows that multi-tasking really doesn't save time; you lose time when you switch from one task to another, resulting in a loss of productivity. Routine multi-tasking can also lead to difficulty in concentrating when you need to focus.

Cut down on interruptions...but be flexible. It's a good habit to allow yourself some private time during the day, where you close your door and it's understood that you are not to be interrupted. Try not to schedule more than three-quarters of your day so that you have time for planning, reflection—and, yes, interruptions.

Learn to say no. Delegate, delegate. Return those monkeys we talked about in Chapter 7 to their rightful owners.

Stay Connected with the "Important"

Remember Eisenhower's rules about dealing with important versus unimportant tasks? One way to stay connected with the important is to create a written life plan and review it on a regular basis. Think of it as a companion to your organization's vision and strategic plan, only it's designed to help you reach your personal and professional goals.

There are many resources for writing a personal life plan. We like the work of Michael Hyatt and highly recommend his blog and books.

A life plan begins with identifying your personal values and then setting goals that align with those values. It is very similar to the work we described in Chapter 2 where we talked about how an organization's core values shape its culture. Think of your life plan as a personal core values statement with goals attached and a plan for achieving those goals.

For a life plan to work, though, you need to write it down (most people resist doing that), and you need to review it. We suggest looking at your plan on a weekly basis, alongside your calendar; then carve out a day each quarter to really focus on reviewing and improving your plan.

At the end of the year, give yourself some downtime to do an annual review and assessment. Block out the coming year by looking ahead a year or two. Are you still focused on what's most important in your life? If not, what do you need to change? As you work through your life plan, you'll find the important tasks fall into place, and the unimportant ones end up on your ignore list.

Dan's Keys to Success

How many meetings do you attend in a week? If you're like me, a lot!

The Harvard Business School and London School of Economics looked at the schedules of more than 500 CEOs and found, on average, that they spent one-third of their time in meetings (and that didn't count phone calls, conference calls and business lunches).

The CEOs themselves, *The Wall Street Journal* reported, were surprised to learn how many hours they were in meetings!

So how do you ensure that your meeting time is well spent?

First, evaluate whether you need to have a meeting in the first place. Don't schedule a meeting unless it is necessary and has a specific purpose.

Second, prepare an agenda and stick to it. As Stephen Covey used to say, "Begin with the end in mind." Inform participants of the purpose of the meeting and what they need to be prepared to discuss or decide. Provide handouts ahead of time.

Third, start your meetings on time, and end them on time.

Fourth, keep informational meetings short and to the point, especially if they are designed simply to update participants.

Fifth, delegate someone on your staff to attend meetings you do not need to attend personally. You really don't need to "sit in" every meeting.

Sixth, prepare minutes or a summary, with action steps, immediately after a meeting, and circulate them to the participants.

Anthony's Takeaways

Is exercise part of your daily routine? If it isn't, it should be.

Mason Currey, author of *Daily Rituals: How Artists Work*, discovered that many famous artists made a habit of taking daily walks. Composers, in particular, liked to take walks.

Beethoven, Mahler and Satie all took walks. Tchaikovsky, Currey writes, "believed he had to take a walk of exactly two hours a day and that if he returned even a few minutes early, great misfortunes would befall him."

You don't have to be away from your desk for two hours to enjoy the health benefits of walking. Just 30 minutes a day can literally save your life.

Studies have shown that walking 30 minutes daily can increase cardiovascular fitness, strengthen bones, reduce excess body fat, and boost muscle power and endurance. It can also reduce your risk of developing heart disease, type 2 diabetes, osteoporosis and some cancers.

Walking gets you out of your work surroundings, especially if you walk outdoors. It clears your head and helps you focus. Studies also show that walking results in a better night's sleep, decreases stress, improves your memory and boosts your mood.

One study found that the more steps people took during the day, the better their moods were. Now there's an incentive!

At NAFCU, we started a walking club a few years ago. I highly recommend that you make walking part of your routine.

CHAPTER TEN

Having Fun

"A sense of humor is part of the art of leadership, of getting along with people, of getting things done."
– Dwight D. Eisenhower

You're in a meeting, and the discussion is going nowhere. Everyone's suggestions are falling flat. Out of the blue, someone cracks a joke. It's not a knee-slapper, but it breaks the tension, and suddenly fresh ideas are flowing. The mood has changed, and now you're getting somewhere.

If you're like us, you enjoy a good laugh and having fun at work. Humor just seems to make the day go better. In fact, research shows that humor boosts morale, builds relationships and improves teamwork. Fun and laughter are also known to make you feel good, reduce stress, cope with problems, and promote creativity and problem solving.

That being said, the folks at The Financial Brand website surveyed bank and credit union core value statements a few years ago and found only two credit unions that included "fun." Not a single bank made the "fun" list.

"What's sad about this is that only two financial institutions out of 100 believe in *Fun*," wrote The Financial Brand. "Financial services are as boring as it gets," they chided. "It's too bad more banks and credit unions don't see the opportunity to make banking more pleasant and entertaining for both consumers and employees alike."

Making Fun a Part of Your Culture

We beg to differ. We know plenty of credit unions that have incorporated fun into their workplace culture. While it may not make their core values statement, many credit unions are making it a priority in hiring. Here's just one example we saw on a credit union's website:

> *"We need fun people. Our people can provide positive energy in any situation with their optimistic attitude. We are always seeking the best in people."*

We also know lots of credit union CEOs who have a playful side to their personality. One CEO we know dresses up as Santa Claus on Christmas Eve and drives around in an open car. Another is in a rock band. One dresses in her pajamas on Pajama Day. Yes, even numbers people can have fun.

One of the most celebrated fun places to work is Southwest Airlines, which we talked about in Chapter 4 on hiring for attitude. Former CEO Herb Kelleher once said, "What we are looking for, first and foremost, is a sense of humor. We don't care much about education and expertise because we can train people. We hire attitudes." During job interviews, candidates at Southwest are asked to give an example of how they've recently used their sense of humor on the job and how they've "used humor to defuse a difficult situation."

Technology companies and dot-com startups have long been known for providing fun activities for their employees, from beach volleyball and bowling at Google to foosball and Ping-Pong at LinkedIn. In fact, the Googleplex, Google's headquarters in Mountain View, Calif., looks more like an adult playground than a corporate office.

The Benefits of Fun

Jerry Greenfield, cofounder of Ben & Jerry's, is famous for saying, "If it's not fun, why do it?" Put another way, why *not* have fun if it's good for you and your organization? We summarized some of the benefits of humor at the beginning of the chapter. Now let's take a closer look at a few of them.

Humor reduces stress. Stress is one of the main causes of illness, absenteeism and burnout. Humor is a great stress reliever because it makes us feel good. It triggers the release of endorphins, the body's "feel-good" chemical. It also boosts energy and diminishes pain.

Laughter is good for your body. Laughter relieves physical tension, relaxing your muscles for up to 45 minutes. It increases immune cell function and infection-fighting antibodies. And, it's heart-healthy because it increases blood flow.

Humor boosts social skills. Laughter is universal—it cuts across cultures and nationalities. Scientists believe that laughter allows humans to connect, bond and communicate with one another.

Humor provides perspective. Jokes offer a new and different take on a situation. They force you to see in new ways as your brain interprets a seemingly incongruous ending or punch line. "Empathic" humor enables us to have compassion for someone or a situation outside our normal frame of reference.

Humor makes us more creative and productive. Laugher releases dopamine into our brains, heightening creativity, productivity and engagement. Studies have shown that happy employees have higher productivity and sales rates.

Humor fosters teamwork. Humor facilitates trust, eases tension and establishes group cohesion. Business teams that have fun solve problems faster and get higher customer service ratings.

Lighten Up to Boost Productivity

As the old saying goes, "Laughter is the best medicine." Scientists are learning more and more that laughter has immense therapeutic benefits. And more and more CEOs are learning that fun can have tremendous business benefits as well.

"To the great surprise of many CEOs, helping employees lighten up on the job has boosted productivity at the same time that it has provided an invaluable skill in coping with ever-increasing levels of job stress," writes Paul McGhee, a Ph.D. researcher on laughter. "While humor and fun are generally not mentioned in the context of Total Quality Management, they are essential to getting employees to 'internalize' the commitment to quality."

There's no doubt about it, lightening up can pay dividends in increased morale, productivity and teamwork at your credit union.

Here are some ideas we've gathered for injecting some fun into your workday. Many of them you may already do. If you don't, give them a try.

Contests. Contests to name new products or services, charities you will support or new ideas to better serve your members are a great way to boost morale and get the creative juices flowing.

Off-site get-togethers. Invite your team to go off-site with you to brainstorm an idea or solve a problem. At the bowling alley, miniature golf course or go-cart racetrack, you'll have a chance to loosen up and come up with ideas that you probably never would have thought of in a conference room.

Dress-up or -down days. Set aside days where your staff can dress to a theme, whether it's the '70s, Halloween or the movies.

Break room. Do you have a break or staff room where employees can relax? Make the break room a "fun zone" by allowing employees to put jokes or funny stories on the bulletin board, play games, or put up inspirational posters or artwork they've made.

Intranet/newsletter. Use your Intranet or employee newsletter to feature amusing stories and jokes from your employees.

Staff meetings. Start or end your staff meetings with something fun. It could be a drawing for a t-shirt, an amusing award that you give out each month or just something silly.

Share a lunch. Start a lunch (or breakfast) club where everyone brings a dish, or periodically invite someone on your staff to have lunch with you.

Walking or exercise club. Get the blood flowing and conversation going! See Anthony's Takeaways in Chapter 9.

Music night out. There's nothing like singing karaoke in front of your employees or doing a line dance. Give it a try!

Birthdays and special occasions. If you don't already, make it a point to celebrate birthdays and employee milestones.

Special days. From Valentine's Day to the Fourth of July, make it "okay" to have themed activities on these special days.

Company picnic. Combine good food with plenty of activities for all ages and levels at your annual get-together.

Civic activities. Credit unions are involved in many causes. Make it a fun, group activity.

Dan's Keys to Success

Thankfully, performing standup comedy isn't in the job description for most leadership positions. But when we do hear a good quip or zinger from a CEO, it's memorable, isn't it?

Good leaders are actually pretty good humorists. They know that humor is an effective way to relieve tension, motivate people or make key points stick.

So what cues can we take from standup comedy? Plenty, it turns out. Here are a few one-liners you should include in your next gig:

Be humble. Humor and humility go hand-in-hand. I love this quip from Warren Buffett: "I buy expensive suits. They just look cheap on me." Leaders need to get over themselves.

Timing is everything. Like a good salesman closing a deal, a standup comedian knows when to get to the punch line. Pace and timing are crucial to making effective presentations and holding your audience's attention.

Watch what I do, not what I say. Comedians live or die by how well they read an audience and how they use their body language. Leaders need to master nonverbal cues, too. How you "look" may be more important than the words you say. By the same token, pay attention to the nonverbal signals your team may be sending you.

It takes courage to go out there. Think of the chutzpah it takes to step onto a stage and "knock 'em dead." Leaders must have courage, too—to face an unfriendly audience, deliver bad news or be the voice of confidence when, in reality, there is chaos all around.

Anthony's Takeaways

Ordinarily, I'm a pretty jovial person. But as a former "compliance guy," I have to get serious for a moment and caution against the dark (and quite possibly actionable) side of humor.

It's great to have fun at work, but it's also important to follow some basic rules of the road so your credit union doesn't find itself on the wrong side of a lawsuit.

Here are some commonsense guidelines to keep in mind:

- Make sure fun is appropriate for the workplace.
- Use humor to lift people up, not put them down.
- Use humor to put people at ease, not single them out or make them feel awkward.
- Make fun inclusive, not exclusive.
- Be sensitive to how people will react. What is fun for one person may not be fun for another. Be very careful with sarcasm; it can easily be taken the wrong way.

Here are the no-no's. Workplace fun should never:

- Be racist, sexist, disrespectful or vulgar,
- Be offensive,
- Make fun of an individual,
- Detract from the credit union's core business,
- Damage the reputation of individuals or
- Damage the reputation of the credit union.

What's the safest humor you can practice? Self-deprecating humor. Laugh at yourself, not others. Poking fun at yourself shows you're human.

CHAPTER ELEVEN

A Balanced Life

"Be a life long or short, its completeness
depends on what it was lived for."
– DAVID STARR JORDAN

What's important in your life?

Most executives aren't much for "contemplating their navels." That kind introspection gets pushed aside in favor of doing things.

After all, it was Carl Jung who said, "You are what you do, not what you say you'll do." So perhaps a better way of asking the question is, "What do you like to do?"

What do you do in your spare time or on vacation? Or what would you do if you took a one-year sabbatical?

Maybe you are doing exactly what want and your life is complete. If that's the case, we say wonderful!

But if you have this nagging suspicion that your life could be better balanced, read on.

The "Whole Person" Approach to Life

In 1961, Mortimer J. Adler, the philosopher and educator who started the Great Books Foundation, spoke at the annual meeting of the Million Dollar Round Table. MDRT is an organization for the top producers in the life insurance field, so the audience that day was comprised of the nation's most successful agents. What could Adler say to them that would make a difference in their busy lives?

In a nutshell, he challenged these highly motivated business people to live their lives more fully by paying attention to seven key areas: relationships, health, education, career, service, finances and spirituality. To its credit, MDRT embraced Adler's message and has made the whole-person concept a part of its program ever since.

As MDRT puts it:

> *"With all the demands for your time and attention, it is easy to lose touch with the other equally important aspects of your life—family, community*

service, health and spirituality. To bring all those elements into balance, many MDRT members have embraced the Whole Person concept.

"Living a well-rounded, balanced lifestyle and becoming a Whole Person is the foundation for:

- *Ongoing happiness,*
- *Loving family relationships,*
- *Strong friendships,*
- *Self-confidence,*
- *Good health,*
- *Financial security and*
- *Intellectual fulfillment."*

Spending some time reflecting on each of these areas is a good "reality check" to see where you are with your life's priorities. According to Adler, "Whole Persons are engaged in a lifetime quest to achieve balance and congruity in all aspects of their lives and continually seek to develop their full human potential."

The "Wheel of Life"

If you've ever listened to a motivational tape or read a "success" book, you've probably heard of Paul J. Meyer, the founder of Success Motivation Institute. Meyer was a member of MDRT in the early 1960s and came up with the popular "Wheel of Life" concept used by many life and career coaches to help clients put their lives into perspective.

Meyer divided a wheel or circle into the six sections of a balanced life:

- Family and Home
- Financial and Career
- Physical and Health
- Spiritual and Ethical
- Mental and Educational
- Social and Cultural

You can use your own categories, based on your individual goals or life stage. Regardless, the approach is the same. Each category gets assigned a numerical value (1–10, with 10 being the highest). You then plot the numbers on the wheel, along an axis starting at the center (1) of the circle and moving to its outermost ring (10).

If you're familiar with radar or "spider" charts, you'll know what we're talking about. For example, if you spend a lot of time at work, the Career category might be assigned a 10. If you haven't exercised lately or have gained some weight, Health might be rated only a 2.

As you plot each category and connect the dots, it quickly becomes apparent which areas of your life are "out of balance." They are the ones that either stick way out or are barely noticeable on the wheel.

It's not likely that you will have a perfectly balanced wheel. At times your career will be demanding; at other times, you may need to care for an elderly parent or spend time with your children. The circle helps you see where you are. Then you can decide what the ideal level is for each category and begin working towards changing those areas in your life that need attention.

Work-life Balance: Is It Possible?

It really boils down to making life choices, doesn't it? Jack Welch put it this way: "There's no such thing as work-life balance. There are work-life choices, and you make them, and they have consequences."

We always have a choice, although at times it doesn't seem that way. Take Erin Callan, the CFO at Lehman Brothers before it collapsed. She wrote a bittersweet piece in *The New York Times* about the price she paid for putting her career ahead of family, friends and first husband. "I didn't start out with the goal of devoting all of myself to my job," she wrote. "It crept in over time...My boundaries slipped away until work was all that was left."

We've all had those times when our work has over-taken us, especially if we are up against a big dead-line. But to have those times become the norm isn't very healthy. How do you keep your boundaries from slipping away, though?

It's not always easy, but as we discussed in Chapters 7 and 9 (Accountability and Time Management), you learn to set some limits.

Executives who successfully juggle personal and work life say one of their secrets is to schedule down-time. Put vacations on your calendar at the begin-ning of each year. This gives you a goal to work to-wards, and it also ensures that you actually take a vacation.

Jeff Weiner, the CEO of LinkedIn, also recommends building breaks or "buffers" into each day, time peri-ods that you purposely keep clear of meetings so you can think and "catch your breath."

"Use that buffer time to think big, catch up on the latest industry news, get out from under that pile of unread emails, or just take a walk," Weiner says. "Whatever you do, just make sure you make that time for yourself—everyday and in a system-atic way—and don't leave unscheduled moments to chance."

Sir Richard Branson, the celebrated CEO of Virgin, has often said that his family comes first. Book time to spend with your family, Branson urges. Rather than thinking of work and family as mutually exclusive, Branson says you should combine the two. "As I've often said," he writes in *Entrepreneur* magazine, "I don't divide work and play: It's all living."

Having Passion for Your Life's Work

Psychologists have long noted that when people have a passion for their work, they are happier and more fulfilled. In a *Harvard Business Review* blog post, Tomas Chamorro-Premuzic, an expert on psychometric testing and professor of business psychology at University College London, suggests that engagement is the difference between the bright and dark side of "workaholism."

"Work is just like a relationship," he writes. "Spending one week on a job that you hate is as dreadful as spending a week with a person you don't like. But when you find the right job, or the right person, no amount of time is enough. Do what you love and you will love what you do, which will also make you love working harder and longer."

Interestingly, researchers at Harvard recently completed five years of interviews with almost 4,000 executives worldwide to find out how they reconcile their professional and personal lives.

The upshot of their research was not so much a picture of balance but of senior executives who had learned to make deliberate choices about their careers, combining work and home, and effectively involving their families in their work decisions.

Authors Boris Groysberg and Robin Abrahams, in a *Harvard Business Review* article, identified five themes that emerged from their research. Successful executives, they said, have learned to: define success for themselves, manage technology, build support networks at work and at home, travel or relocate selectively and collaborate with their partner.

Get a Life

Most successful CEOs, we have found, have figured out how to "get a life." They take vacations. They have interesting hobbies. They are physically fit. They spend time with their children. How do they do it?

Here are a few tips we've gleaned from observing those who have their act together:

Remove those things that sap or waste your time. Eliminate time-wasters and avoid situations and people that have a high level of negativity.

Surround yourself and hire people with a positive, "can-do" attitude.

Set new goals and try new things. Lifelong learning isn't just for your professional life. Challenge yourself by learning to play an instrument, fly a plane, climb a mountain or cook a gourmet meal. You'll develop new skills and stay young!

Take care of yourself. It goes without saying, but make sure you get plenty of sleep, eat well and exercise regularly. Nothing affects your mood or ability to function more than your health. (See Anthony's Takeaways.)

Get rid of clutter. Simplify your life so that you have the space and time to focus on what's important.

Form an accountability group. It could be family, friends or colleagues, but create a support group where you hold each other mutually accountable for personal and professional goals.

Unplug from email and social media. Set boundaries for when you reply to emails at night or on weekends. Unplug from social media to spend time with family. When on vacation, don't be on email all day long.

Delegate. Learn to delegate so that you can step away and not be worried about whether tasks are completed. Give your staff a chance to flex their leadership muscles, too.

Recharge your batteries. Schedule time during the year to completely get away and unwind. It could be riding your motorcycle in the Great Smoky Mountains, rafting down the Colorado River or lying on the beach at Waikiki. Relax, recharge and reconnect!

Expect the unexpected. Life happens. Kids get sick. Your flight gets canceled. A flood destroys one of your branch offices. Be flexible and take life in stride.

Just say no. Say no to what's not important, so you can say yes to what is.

Dan's Keys to Success

A lot of managers cringe when they hear "work-life balance." Uh-oh, here comes a request to work at home, leave early or miss an important meeting because of family obligations.

If you have a flexible approach to work-life issues, though, your organization should be able to handle these kinds of situations as they arise.

Studies have shown that work-life balance initiatives can:

- Reduce absenteeism,
- Increase productivity,
- Improve morale and working relationships,
- Decrease stress and burnout,
- Attract new employees and
- Help retain current employees.

In designing a work-life balance policy, it's best to survey your employees and get their input. Understanding changing workplace demographics helps as well.

Sometimes work-life balance can be as simple as allowing flexibility in work hours to accommodate daycare or eldercare schedules. Or allowing time off for doctor's appointments and personal errands.

Giving employees permission to "unplug" in their off hours cuts down on stress as well. For example, you might establish a policy that no one is expected to reply to an email at night or on weekends, unless it's urgent.

Anthony's Takeaways

There are so many things in our busy lives that are outside of our control. But the wonderful thing is this—the list of things we *can* control includes three very important areas.

I call them life's springboards—sleep, exercise and a healthy diet.

When you get all three working for you, the results are amazing. Would nailing all three take work off our plate? Nope. But I believe it would allow you to get more done and get it done better.

So, here are three simple questions:

1. *Are you getting enough sleep?* Research puts that number between seven and eight hours.
2. *Are you getting enough exercise?* Amazing things happen when you can get as little as 20 to 30 minutes a day.
3. *Is your diet where it should be?*

As I look at this list, I can honestly answer no to each question. Now, I've made improvements with exercise and diet, but I'm not where I should be. Sleep? Don't get me started.

And I'd bet dollars to ~~donuts~~ carrot sticks that if I nailed all three, the rest of my life would improve—dramatically.

And here's another thought. If you agree with me that sleep, exercise and a good diet are life's springboards, what should we be doing in our organizations to promote all three?

Conclusion

In our introduction, we talked about the need for credit union leaders—everyone, really—to learn and practice good people skills. Leading and managing well, we said, ain't rocket science, but it's still hard work.

We then made the case for embracing change and creating organizations that have strong core values, vibrant cultures and a clear vision. We talked about how important it is to hire for attitude, and we encouraged you to build collaborative teams that can adapt and innovate.

We asked you to look in the mirror and take a hard look at yourself and your organization. Are you leading as well as you could? Are you setting an example for your people? And, by the way, we ask ourselves those same questions—often. Just because we wrote a book doesn't mean we get off the hook.

We laid out for you what we think are essential leadership traits: communication, trust, accountability, integrity, compassion, humility and humor. We stressed the importance of continuous learning and feedback, taking risks, using time wisely, balancing work and life, and having fun.

Make a commitment to learning, we said. Steady improvement, practice and the discipline of a Ben Franklin or Thomas Edison will make you a better leader, team member, parent or volunteer.

We never claimed to be rocket scientists, far from it. Our goal has been to provide you with a simple, straightforward guide and inspire you to better serve your members.

However, we can't resist one reference to rocket science before we leave you. It's something called "max Q," and, no, we didn't make it up.

Max Q is the point at which aerodynamic stress on a vehicle is at its maximum. Rockets and missiles can only withstand max Q for a limited time or they will sustain structural damage.

You might recall that during a space shuttle flight, the main engines were throttled back to about 70 percent at around 35,000 feet. This was to prevent the breaking up of the shuttle as it reached max Q.

There is even an equation for max Q:

$$q = \frac{1}{2}pv^2$$

Don't ask us to explain it because we can't. That's for another book.

But here's our takeaway (and it ain't rocket science):

There will always be limitations.

And there will always be ways **around** *those limitations.*

In the late 1950s, there were those who categorically dismissed the notion of manned space flights to the moon. Impossible, they said. Too many obstacles. Too many unknowns.

> *"To place a man in a multi-stage rocket and project him into the controlling gravitational field of the moon where the passengers can make scientific observations, perhaps land alive, and then return to earth—all that constitutes a wild dream worthy of Jules Verne. I am bold enough to say that such a man-made voyage will never occur regardless of all future advances."*
>
> – Lee De Forest, American radio pioneer
> and inventor of the vacuum tube (1957)

In Chapter 2, though, we talked about having a Big, Hairy, Audacious Goal (BHAG). A wonderful thing happens when you have a BHAG. Things get done. Impossible odds don't seem so impossible. Determined and dedicated teams rally around a shared, audacious goal, and they overcome obstacles.

As Michael Jordan once said, "Obstacles don't have to stop you. If you run into a wall, don't turn around and give up. Figure out how to climb it, go through it or work around it."

There will always be Lee De Forests—people who tell you that it can't be done. Visionary leaders don't listen to that kind of talk. Instead, they inspire others to stretch towards their goals, no matter how unreachable they may seem. They persevere despite the obstacles.

Friends, don't let max Q keep your rocket on the launch pad. Don't let obstacles hold back your dreams and aspirations. Blast off!

If you apply yourself as we've suggested in this book, there ain't nothing that can stop you.